D0795934

RHINO

EVERYTHING YOU KNOW IS WRONG

BY PAUL KIRCHNER

GENERAL PUBLISHING GROUP
Los Angeles

Publisher: W. Quay Hays
Editor: Harold Bronson
Managing Editor: Colby Allerton
Art Director: Nadeen Torio
Color and Pre-Press Director: Gaston Moraga
Production Assistants: Tom Archibeque, Allan Peak

© 1995 by Rhino Records

All rights reserved under International and
Pan-American Copyright Conventions.
This book, or any parts thereof, may not be
reproduced in any fashion whatsoever without
the prior written permission of the publisher.

For information:
General Publishing Group, Inc.
2701 Ocean Park Boulevard, Suite 140
Santa Monica, CA 90405

Library of Congress Catalog Card Number 95-081721

Printed in the USA
10 9 8 7 6 5 4 3 2 1

General Publishing Group
Los Angeles

CONTENTS

We hope we're not wrong in prognosticating that if you enjoy this book, you're sure to delight in the pages of other Rhino Books published by GPG.

Forgotten Fads and Fabulous Flops

This book's author, Paul Kirchner's previous book that *Boomer* magazine critiqued as "a wonderful, heavily illustrated bundle of fun." A re-introduction to famous American can't misses: the Edsel, the Susan B. Anthony dollar and 3-D movies, as well as more unbelievable and esoteric rages that just didn't last. Remember Goldfish Swallowing, the Drinking Man's Diet and the Topless Swimsuit?

The Best of the World's Worst

The world's worst army, the world's worst state to live in, the world's worst animal sex maniacs…it's all here in this 192 page collection compiled by Marvel's Stan Lee. The *National Enquirer* described it as "Hilarious blunders and side-splitting stories."

Va Va Voom!

The first truly comprehensive account of the breathtaking glamour girls from the 1940s and '50s—pioneers such as Mamie Van Doren, Lili St. Cyr, June Wilkinson, Stella Stevens, Blaze Starr, Candy Barr and others, as well as icons Monroe, Mansfield and Bardot—compellingly told in their own words, and jammed with photographs.

If your local bookstore is too unhip to have these treasures continually in stock, call Rhino's mail order department at 1-800-432-0020. While you're at it, have the customer service rep send you Rhino's latest comprehensive catalogue if you're interested in checking out what *Spin* magazine and others have called "America's Best Record Label" has to offer. Toot! Toot!

INTRODUCTION

Okay, not everything. My research was unable to establish that the Egyptian pyramids were built by Italian craftsmen in the eighteenth century; that gum chewing makes you look intelligent; or that, though Regis and Kathie Lee are a man and a woman, it is Regis who is the woman. Nevertheless, it is surprising how much of what we take for granted turns out to be wrong. In the course of a week, you're almost certain to hear one of the fallacies included in this book. Some are bits of folk wisdom or old wives' tales that don't hold up. There are the misquotes—the most commonly repeated quotations are often misstated or mistakenly attributed. Some are fallacies we believe because we've seen them with our own eyes—at least, we've seen them in the movies. There is our national mythology. There are logical assumptions, the logic of which most of us have never questioned. There are any number of things that we accept because they sound as though they should be true, whether or not they are.

Why should you care? Two reasons.

The first is noble. Truth is beauty, knowledge is its own reward and learning things is one of life's great delights. Not only that, but you can't set out on your quest for the Meaning of Life with a brain cluttered with a lot of nonsense. You want to make sure that the premises upon which you operate are, as far as possible, factual.

Which brings us to the second reason—the dark side. Knowledge is power. We educate ourselves for the same reason the streetfighter polishes his moves—we want to be top dog. Do you want to be the one at a gathering who passes along a commonplace belief, only to suffer the humiliation of being corrected by someone who knows better? Or do you want to be the one in the position of holding that ill-informed person's fate in your hands? If it's someone whose friendship you want to cultivate, you can deliver a modest but masterful elucidation, exciting speculation as to the hitherto unsuspected breadth and depth of your knowledge. If it's your obnoxious brother-in-law, why not demolish him?

But be careful. Nothing is so changeable as the truth, I learned, as I reviewed similar collections of misconceptions published in the past, and noticed that a number of their pronouncements have themselves been misconceived. I've not included any topics on which the experts seem to have any serious differences of opinion, but facts may surface that will prove some of the things in this book wrong. So I set out boldly to debunk, yet realize that I too may be caught in error. It goes with the territory.

ACKNOWLEDGMENTS

The following were kind enough to lend their expertise to the compilation of this book: Tom Conroy, Movie Still Archives, Harrison, Nebraska; The Staff of The Miller Library, Hamden, Connecticut; Col. Jeff Cooper; Finn Aagaard; Brian Smith and Bruce Barber, WPLR, Hamden, Connecticut; William Fischer, M.D.; John Kirchner, M.D.; David Pinkert, D.M.D.; Armand Morgan, Peabody Museum, New Haven, Connecticut; Scott Buttfield; Agency for International Development; International Red Cross; Pete Sepp at the National Taxpayers Union; Lori Tietz at the National Safety Council; Center for Disease Control; Kevin Holloway at the American Petroleum Institute; National Transportation Safety Board; American Plastics Council; Ralph Insinga of the Baseball Hall of Fame; Steve Iacoviello, Olin Chemical; Bob Jackson, Huron Tech; Christian Butzky, University of California at Davis, Department of Viticulture and Enology; David Rabinowitz, Ph.D.; Don Nichols, The U.S. Mint; Larry Hama; Harold Bronson; Joni Solomon; Colby Allerton; and Neil Werde, who got the ball rolling.

Readers with amusing examples of flops, blunders, and misconceived notions are invited to send them to the author through the General Publishing Group, 2701 Ocean Park Blvd., Suite 140, Santa Monica, CA 90405. Verifiable contributions will be acknowledged and may be included in future compilations, with attribution.

TO MY PARENTS

ABNER DOUBLEDAY INVENTED
BASEBALL AT COOPERSTOWN IN 1839

Abner Doubleday was a fine American. A graduate of West Point, he
served in the Mexican War and was a Civil War hero who fired the
first shot at the Confederates from Fort Sumter. He achieved the
rank of general and later became a writer; mastered French, Spanish
and Sanskrit; and obtained the charter for San Francisco's first cable
car. Of course, his immortality was assured when he was recognized
as having invented the American national pastime at Cooperstown,
New York, in 1839. Unfortunately this could have given him little
satisfaction, since at the time of his death he had no idea he had done
so. There is no evidence that Doubleday ever played a game of baseball, or even watched one. Nowhere in his writings does he mention
the game, and in 1839 he wasn't even *in* Cooperstown.

Two hundred and fifty years ago, the British were playing a
game called Rounders on a diamond with a base at each corner,
usually a stone or a post. A "pecker" or "feeder" pitched a ball to a
"striker," who tried to hit it with a bat. If the striker hit the ball
over the diamond, he could "round" the square, running and
touching the four corner markers in succession for a point. He was
out if he missed three pitches, hit a foul ball or hit a fly that was
caught. This game was often referred to as "baseball." It is probably what Jane Austen had in mind when, in her 1798 novel
Northanger Abbey, she wrote that the heroine would rather play
cricket and "baseball" than study. The main difference between this
game and what we now call baseball is that a fielded ball could be
thrown at the base runner in order to make an out.

In the 1840s a New York City bank clerk named Alexander
Cartwright and his friends set up the Knickerbocker Base Ball
Club, which established most of the finer points of the game. The
diamond was established as 90 feet per side, teams as having nine
players each and the innings ending after three outs. In 1849
Cartwright traveled to California and popularized his version of the
game around the country. Harold Peterson's *The Man Who
Invented Baseball* calls Cartwright the true father of the game.

So how did Abner Doubleday, Cooperstown and 1839 figure
into all this? It was all a plot by a giant corporation, as you might
have suspected. Around the turn of the century, A. G. Spalding, the
sports equipment manufacturer, was disturbed by suggestions that

the all-American game of baseball had a British pedigree. In 1907 he set about finding an American inventor for the game. Spalding felt this would benefit the image of the sport, not to mention the sales of sports equipment. On the basis of a letter received from an Abner Graves, an octogenarian who had been raised in upstate New York, the honor was given to Doubleday. Spalding was particularly taken with the idea that the father of baseball would also have had a distinguished military career.

In 1939, the game's centennial, the Baseball Hall of Fame was opened in Cooperstown to celebrate Doubleday's achievement, which would no doubt have pleased and perplexed Mr. Doubleday himself.

ABORTION WAS ILLEGAL THROUGH MOST OF OUR HISTORY

Many people assume that prior to *Roe v. Wade*, the 1973 Supreme Court case that overturned laws prohibiting abortion, the procedure had always been illegal except in the more liberal states that had changed their laws. Legal scholars question whether there is anything in the Constitution that can be said to permit abortion, but at the time the Constitution was written the procedure was not against the law. The United States had no anti-abortion laws until the 1820s, when several states passed laws prohibiting abortion after quickening (the baby's first movement) and even then, only when poisons were used. By the 1840s, 10 states had outlawed the procedure. Before that time it was not known how the embryo was formed; prior to research with the microscope, the egg produced by the woman had not been identified. Only with the realization that the sperm fertilized the egg was it understood that there was a "moment of conception." Everyone had previously assumed that the male sperm somehow developed into a recognizable human being roughly four months after intercourse, when the mother felt the quickening.

Other states gradually passed stronger laws, which mostly went unenforced, but the nineteenth century had ended by the time abortion was generally outlawed. Even so, it is estimated that in the second half of the nineteenth century there was one abortion for every half-dozen live births. Pressure to criminalize abortion came not from religious groups but from the medical community, which was then trying to establish professional standards that would set doctors apart from midwives and folk practitioners.

ADAM AND EVE ATE AN APPLE BECAUSE A SNAKE TEMPTED THEM

Ridding the world of misconceptions is a hopeless task—they go as far back as Adam and Eve. Contrary to what you may have heard...

There is no reference to a snake in the Garden of Eden, only to a serpent. In Biblical parlance, a serpent could be any crawling thing. As punishment for tempting Adam and Eve, God condemned it to spend eternity crawling on its belly in the dust, which wouldn't make much sense if it had no legs to begin with.

It probably wasn't an apple that Eve gave Adam. The only reference in the Bible is to the "fruit of the tree" (Gen. 3:3). It is unlikely that apples would grow in the part of the world in which we would expect to find a garden of Eden. In order to produce top-quality fruit, apple trees require longer periods of cold weather than a couple of naked people would be willing to put up with. A fig is more likely, especially since Adam and Eve covered themselves with fig leaves when they lost their innocence.

Many people assume that Adam and Eve had only two children, which would leave an awful lot unexplained. Gen. 4:1-2 names three sons: Cain, Abel and Seth; Gen. 5:4 indicates that Adam went on to father an unspecified number of sons and daughters.

One of the strangest beliefs that the story of Adam and Eve has engendered is that men have one less rib than women because God took a rib from Adam to create Eve. The most cursory inventory would indicate that each sex has a full set of 12 pairs.

THE AIR FORCE IS WHERE THE PLANES ARE

Since the United States Air Force was made into a separate branch of the armed services in 1947 (it had formerly been part of the army), it would be logical to assume that the air force is where the planes are. Logical—but that would overlook the dynamics of inter-service rivalry. Aware that military aircraft are the sexiest draw for recruits, the army and the navy have both made sure they have their fair share. You may have noticed that nearly every navy recruiting poster features a jet taking off from an aircraft carrier rather than a swabbie greasing a propeller shaft six decks below. Surprisingly, though, it is the army that has the most aircraft of any branch of the armed forces. As of April 1995, it lists 7,900, including helicopters and light reconnaissance craft, to the air force's 6,815 and the navy and marines' combined force of 5,019.

AN AIRPLANE'S BLACK BOX IS BLACK

Every military and commercial plane carries a "black box," which records flight data and cockpit conversations. It is retrieved after an accident in order to learn what went wrong. Though called a black box, it is actually bright orange. After a serious accident it may end up some distance from the wreckage, so there wouldn't be much point in making it any harder to spot than necessary.

IN AMERICA, THE MAJORITY RULES

Nothing would have been more disconcerting to those who wrote our Constitution than Ross Perot's proposal that issues be decided by a national town hall meeting. The Framers established a number of procedures to limit what they termed "the tyranny of the majority." These include the stipulation that every state gets two senators regardless of population; certain legislation requires two-thirds of the votes in Congress to pass; and the Senate filibuster, which enables a single senator to prevent an issue coming to a vote. The Bill of Rights elaborates individual freedoms that cannot be overruled, and the Supreme Court can overturn laws it deems unconstitutional despite the will of the majority.

The Framers understood that, as an individual, it makes little difference to you whether you are oppressed by a single despot or by the views of the bulk of your fellow citizens—you're still oppressed. Their main concern was with the threat to property. In

1787 John Adams wrote that if the majority were to control all branches of the government, "Debts would be abolished first; taxes laid heavy on the rich, and not at all on others; and at last a downright equal division of everything would be demanded and voted."

THE AMERICAN REVOLUTION WAS FOUGHT AGAINST THE BRITISH, ETC.

Though we are aware that the American colonists were not united in opposition to British rule, most of us do not realize just how disunited they were. John Adams estimated that about a third of the colonists, known as patriots, supported the Revolution; a third, known as loyalists, were opposed to it; and a third didn't care much one way or the other. Almost as many Americans fought against independence as fought for it; in 1780 there were 9,000 patriots in Washington's army and 8,000 loyalists in the British forces. Connecticut, Massachusetts and Virginia were hotbeds of the Revolution, but New York contributed most of its troops to the

British side. George Washington, Thomas Jefferson and Benjamin Franklin all had relatives who fought for the king. In many ways the American Revolution was actually a civil war.

The American Revolution caused nothing like the terror and upheaval of the French Revolution, but countless loyalists were tarred and feathered and had their property confiscated. As many as 100,000 fled to Canada out of a population of 2,500,000, a higher percentage than those who left France.

It is commonly believed that the patriots fought Indian-style against the British, crouching behind trees and picking off the redcoats as they stupidly marched in fixed formations. Presumably the British took this with their customary stiff upper lip, with perhaps a hint of a sneer at the colonials for showing such poor form. In fact, the British had had 75 years of exposure to this type of fighting during the French and Indian Wars, and very little of the Revolution was fought in this fashion. Washington brought in the Prussian Baron Friedrich von Steuben to drill his troops in conventional European tactics, and it was only after mastering them that the patriots were able to defeat the British on the battlefield.

ANIMAL BABIES TOUCHED BY HUMANS WILL BE REJECTED BY THEIR PARENTS

It is widely assumed that after a baby animal is handled by a human, traces of the human scent will cause the wary mother to reject the baby. However, wildlife experts routinely tag or band baby animals without provoking any such reaction. Obviously, a baby animal that is taken from its parents and not returned for a long period may be rejected. (Or one that's been handled by anyone wearing a particularly odious celebrity scent, like *Eau de Michael Jackson*.)

ARABIC NUMBERS CAME FROM ARABIA

"Hindu-Arabic" numbers would be more like it. The "Arabic" numbers we use today were developed in India around A.D. 500, with some of the numerals showing up in Hindu manuscripts dating as far back as 300 B.C. There was a great deal of commerce between Arabia and India, and Arab traders brought the Hindu system back to the Arabic and Persian regions in the mid-eighth century. The numerals themselves were not important—it was the introduction of the decimal system and use of zero that made it a mathematical breakthrough. A Baghdad scholar, Mohammed ibn-Musa al-Khowarizmi, wrote an account of the Hindu system called *Al-jebr wa'l-muqabalah*. (You're not expected to remember that title, but it is interesting that the word "algebra" comes from its first words.) The book was translated into Latin as *De Numero Indorum* ("On the Numbers of the Hindus"), and the new system spread through Europe at the beginning of the twelfth century. Despite the title, Khowarizmi and the Arabs were given credit for the innovation.

The Roman system, which was useless for calculating, was dumped by everyone. Everyone except the movie industry, that is, which found it useful for dating a film's release. In the old days, when it might take a while for prints of a film to make it all over the country, it was advantageous to obscure the date so that audiences wouldn't consider it passé.

Oddly enough, Arabs are among the few peoples in the world who do *not* use Arabic numerals. They have their own set of symbols for numbers, most of which bear no resemblance to those they passed along to the rest of us.

ARMOR WAS SO HEAVY A FALLEN KNIGHT COULD NOT GET UP

A common bit of misinformation is that medieval armor was so heavy that a knight had to be hoisted onto his horse with a derrick, and if he fell off the horse he would be unable to get up off the ground, helpless before the poking spears of his enemies. Although the crude armor of the Romans could weigh as much as 100 pounds, the sophisticated armor of the fifteenth and sixteenth centuries weighed in at about 50 or 60. By comparison, a British SAS commando may go into combat carrying over 200 pounds of equipment and weaponry.

Medieval armor drew most of its strength from meticulous shaping rather than its thickness; it deflected, rather than blocked, direct blows. It was made of numerous small units carefully joined to allow freedom of movement, and with the armor's weight distributed over his entire body, its wearer could run and climb. If he fell down he could easily get up again, provided he wasn't whacked with one of those spiked clubs.

If you've seen armor on display, you may have concluded that the Europeans of a few hundred years ago were seriously altitudinally challenged. They were on average a few inches shorter than us, but

not as short as the armor may make it appear. On the wearer's body the plates were more widely separated than they are in the displays.

AUDUBON WAS AN EARLY
WILDLIFE PRESERVATIONIST

John James Audubon, the nineteenth-century naturalist famous for his detailed paintings of birds, is considered the father of American wildlife conservation. The Audubon Society, founded in 1905 and dedicated to the preservation of wildlife species and their habitats, is named for him. Yet in order to get a close enough look at the subjects of his paintings, Audubon employed a gun. He shot as many as 100 birds in a day. He felt that stuffed birds soon lost their lustrous colors, and that freshly killed ones made better models. Sometimes he required dozens of dead birds to complete a single study.

Audubon did not carry out his carnage with any misgivings—he was an avid and enthusiastic hunter who even shot his share of "buffalo" (more properly "bison"; see "Oh Give Me a Home, Where the Buffalo Roam, and the Deer and the Antelope Play" entry). He foresaw that bison were on the verge of extinction and regretted that possibility, but it didn't bother him enough to stop shooting them.

BANANAS ARE PICKED GREEN SO THAT THEY DON'T SPOIL BEFORE THEY'RE SOLD

It seems logical that bananas are picked green so that they won't spoil before they're sold, but it's not true. They're picked green because they become almost inedible if allowed to ripen on the stalk.

BARBARIANS WERE DESPISED BY THE ROMANS

"Barbarians" has a negative connotation to it, like "Philistine" or "heavy-metal fan." We think of them as those big, hairy, fur-clad types who swept out of Northern Europe and sacked Rome. To the Romans, though, there was nothing pejorative about the term. Any European who wasn't Roman was a barbarian, even if he kept his elbows off the table and always picked up the check. The Romans thought very highly of many barbarians; they came to make up a majority of the Roman army and one was even put in command of it. In his De Germania, the great orator and public official Tacitus wrote that the barbarians possessed an appreciation for personal freedom, an independence of spirit and a love of their land, and that in their culture women were accorded a high status. He favorably contrasted the simple virtue of the barbarians with the moral laxity of the Romans.

Not all barbarians were despised by the Romans.

BASKETBALL PLAYERS SHOOT IN STREAKS AND OTHER APPLICATIONS OF THE LAW OF AVERAGES

Nearly every basketball player, fan and coach believes that a player who makes a few shots has "got the hot hand" and is more likely to hit his next few shots. Similarly, after a player has missed a few shots, he is said to have "gone cold" and is considered more likely to miss the next few times.

Psychologist Thomas Gilovich, professor of psychology at Cornell University, analyzed this common belief in *How We Know What Isn't So: The Fallibility of Human Reason in Everyday Life*. His conclusion? Belief in the "hot hand" is based on a misunderstanding of random sequences.

Gilovich and his colleagues researched the shooting records of the Philadelphia 76ers, the only team that keeps records of the order in which a player's hits and misses occurred. Contrary to popular belief, players were not more likely to make a shot after making their last one—they were more likely to make it after *missing* their last shot. Their chances were even better if they had missed their previous two or three shots. The fact that players, coaches and fans alike continue to believe in shooting streaks is due to their incorrect assumption of what a random sequence should look like. In 20 flips of a coin, there is a 50% chance of getting four heads in a row and a 25% chance of a streak of five. What looks like a run of luck to most people in fact fits within the expected results of a random sequence. The expected 50-50 split only shows up after a sufficient number of tosses, which is why statisticians refer to it as the "law of *large* numbers." It's not unusual for a player to take 20 shots in a game and make 50% of them. Within that 50-50 percentage, though, there is likely to be a run of hits as well as misses. If a player's hits are represented by X's and his misses by O's, his game performance might look like this:

O X X X O X X X O X X O O O X O O X X O O

Though this represents a random sequence, most people who look at it will see evidence of streak shooting. So firmly will people defend the phenomenon that they will interpret the same shot in two different ways, depending on whether they think a player is hot or cold. If he shoots and bounces the ball off the rim while hot, their reaction will be "he almost made it"; the same shot while he's cold will be taken as proof that he can't get it together. The players that Gilovich confronted with his findings refused to accept it, arguing that a hot player cools off because he becomes overconfident and attempts harder shots, or because opponents begin guarding him more carefully. Gilovich disproved this assertion by pointing to "free throw" records—penalty shots taken at the same distance and without defensive pressure. Analyzing statistics from two seasons of Boston Celtic free throws, he found that, on average, the players made 75% of their second shots after making their first and—*surprise!*—75% after missing their first.

The same beliefs about shooting streaks in basketball are found in other areas of life. Gilovich concluded that "people seem compelled to see order, pattern, and meaning in the world, and they find randomness, chaos, and meaninglessness unsatisfying. We tend to 'detect' order where there is none, and to spot meaningful patterns where only the vagaries of chance are operating."

Most gamblers suffer from this misconception. After rolling the dice for a series of even numbers, some will bet that their next throw will produce another even number, expecting their luck to hold out. Others will bet that the next throw will produce an odd number, figuring that the law of averages is working against another even number. To test which theory was more likely, a machine threw dice two million times, and the results were tabulated. After the machine had thrown seven odds in a row, the next toss turned out to be odd 49.85% of the time and even 50.15%. Clearly, there was no pattern one way or the other. No matter what kind of sequence has been set up, the chances of an even or odd total on any particular throw of the dice are always the same—50-50. There is no way to predict the likelihood of a future toss based on the tosses that have gone before.

On several occasions we have heard of lottery winners who have gone on to win the lottery a second time, and the odds against this seem incredible. It should be born in mind that whether or not they have won lotteries in the past, any future tickets they purchase give them the same lousy chances that we all enjoy.

BATS ARE BLIND AND NAVIGATE BY RADAR

The expression "blind as a bat" has been around for centuries, and it doesn't seem so implausible now that we know that bats navigate by radar. Except that they aren't, and don't.

Most species of bats are nocturnal and do not use their eyes very much. However, if forced to leave their dark caves during daylight hours, the bat is capable of seeing once it has adjusted to the glare. The fruit bat and leaf-nosed bat are among the species with quite good vision, and hunt and navigate by sight.

Bats also lack a radar system. *Radar* stands for "radio direction and ranging," and bats do not employ radio waves. They emit high-pitched sounds, which are bounced back to their supersensitive ears. This is closer to *sonar*, or "sound navigation and ranging," though the proper name is *echolocation*. In experiments, a bat's sonar has enabled it to fly around complex obstacles in complete darkness, to avoid a wire the thickness of a hair and to distinguish a flying moth from a variety of similarly shaped objects tossed in the air.

B.C. AND A.D. MARK THE BIRTH OF CHRIST

You may have wondered why the human race counted its years backward until it reached 1 B.C., and then started counting forward. Actually, at that time, the Western world operated under the Roman calendar, and the year we call A.D. 1 was known at the time as the Roman year 754. It didn't acquire its current designation until six centuries later, when it was established by Dionysus Exiguus, a scholarly abbot, as the year of Christ's birth. All that was recorded was that Christ was born near the end of the reign of King Herod. Biblical scholars consider Dionysus' calculations a little off, and place the actual year from as far back as 6 B.C. to as far forward as A.D. 4.

Everyone knows that B.C. is an abbreviation for "Before Christ," and many assume, incorrectly, that A.D. stands for "After Death." It is an abbreviation of the Latin *Anno Domini*, meaning "in the year of our Lord." It wouldn't make much sense otherwise, because we'd have a way to indicate "before" and "after" but not "during." Properly used A.D. appears before rather than after the date it qualifies.

BEARS HIBERNATE THROUGH THE WINTER

Some animals hibernate through the harsh months of winter, their life processes slowed to the minimum. They are deeply unconscious; their body temperature drops and their breathing and heartbeat slow. True hibernators include many fishes, amphibians and reptiles whose body temperature may near freezing during the winter, as well as hedgehogs, ground squirrels and bats. The most common image is of the bear, depicted in cartoons as crawling under the covers and setting his alarm clock to April.

In fact, while bears do sleep through the winter months, they do not actually hibernate. Their metabolism does not slow significantly and they can be easily awakened. Mother bears generally give birth in January and suckle their young during this period. Bears have also developed a neat trick—an anal plug that prevents them from messing up their dens while they sleep. This plug forms naturally from the residue of accumulated vegetable matter and blocks the intestines until it is expelled in the spring. If humans could manage this stunt, it would make the New York subways a lot more inviting.

BEAUTY IS IN THE EYE OF THE BEHOLDER

This is one of those bromides we'd all like to believe in, like "There's someone for everyone." Books such as Naomi Wolf's *The Beauty Myth* have argued that standards of beauty are arbitrary and socially instilled, but this position is hard to defend. Is the Ethiopian supermodel Iman considered homely in her homeland, no match for her cousin with the overbite and the crossedeyes? Unlikely. Most of us agree on who looks good. When *People* names its "Sexiest Man Alive," we know it's more likely to be Brad Pitt than Danny DeVito.

Throughout history, standards of beauty have remained remarkably consistent, except for the concept of the ideal body weight. During the Renaissance, full-figured women were in vogue, particularly with painter Peter Paul Rubens, and "Rubenesque" is still a handy euphemism for the seriously overweight. Rubens' women are not all *that* fat, though—they would be considered fairly fetching by most men today, particularly in a bar at closing time.

In 1987 the University of Texas conducted tests on infants as young as two months old to see if they showed a preference for women's faces that were rated as attractive by adults. Photos of good-looking and plainer-looking people were held in front of the babies, and the babies showed a marked tendency to linger longer over those that were pleasing to the eye. Researcher Judy Langlois felt that her findings "seriously challenge the assumption that attractiveness is merely 'in the eye of the beholder.'"

BELLYBUTTONS—INNIES AND OUTIES ARE DETERMINED BY DOCTORS

Many people believe that whether one ends up with an "innie" or an "outie" bellybutton has something to do with how the doctor ties off the umbilical cord. That theory was put forth by Ian Fleming, who had James Bond wondering whether doctors of France had some special technique that gave French women such perfect navels. Fleming couldn't have paid much attention after his own son was born. It doesn't matter what the doctor does to the part of the umbilical cord that remains attached to the newborn. Within a week it shrivels up and falls off, leaving, randomly, an innie or an outie behind.

BIRDS AREN'T VERY BRIGHT

In the debate about which animal is the smartest—the chimpanzee or the dolphin—the pigeon is often unaccountably left out. One group of animal researchers thought it had uncovered something truly significant when chimpanzees moved boxes in order to be able to reach a bunch of bananas. Shortly afterward, similar tests on specially trained pigeons at Harvard University showed that pigeons were just as capable of meeting the same challenge. Pigeons also performed as well as dolphins when it came to telling the difference between red and green lights in order to get food.

Although the expression "bird brain" is used to suggest a dimwit, the brain of a bird is large and heavy in relation to its body weight, and some birds demonstrate a high degree of intelligence. Seabirds drop shellfish onto rocks in order to break them open. Finches on the Galápagos Islands use cactus spines to probe for insects in crevices. The green heron has been known to place bait in the water, then stand back, wait until fish appear and catch them. A group of ravens in Oregon came up with the idea of picking up stones and dropping them on people who came too close to their nests. Do we expect much more from the average pro-wrestling fan?

BOA CONSTRICTORS CRUSH THEIR PREY

Being crushed to death by a 35-foot-long boa constrictor would rank alongside being gored by a rhinoceros and being torn apart by crocodiles as one of life's less pleasant endings. Actually, it's not as violent as all that. When a boa constrictor wraps a few loops around its prospective dinner, it does not kill its prey by crushing it—it kills it by suffocating it. Every time the prey exhales, the boa constrictor takes up the slack until the victim can no longer breathe at all. Death by boa is less like death by rhino or crocodile than like a bad marriage.

BOGART SAID, "PLAY IT AGAIN, SAM"

These words are familiar to anyone who's seen the classic 1942 film *Casablanca*—yet they were not in the script nor were they spoken in the film. The closest thing to them was Ingrid Bergman's line "Play it, Sam. Play 'As Time Goes By.'" Later, Bogart says, "If she can stand it I can. Play it!" Dooley Wilson, who portrayed Sam, couldn't have played it if he'd wanted to—he didn't know how. He was a drummer. The piano playing was dubbed in under his voice.

When Woody Allen used *Play It Again, Sam* as the title for his homage to Bogart, it was an in-joke—he knew the line was a misquote.

Incidentally, "As Time Goes By" did not make its first appearance in *Casablanca*. It premiered in a 1931 Broadway stage show, *Everybody's Welcome*.

BONES—YOU HAVE THE SAME NUMBER YOUR WHOLE LIFE

It would seem that we would keep the same number of bones, give or take a few, throughout our life. In fact, as babies we have more bones than we do as adults. A baby is born with approximately 350 separate bones, but as it grows many of them fuse together. The skull solidifies, and the last five vertebrae at the end of the backbone join to form a single bony structure, the sacrum. At maturity the average human has 205 bones.

On a different subject, it would seem that a giraffe would have a lot more vertebrae in its neck than would a mouse. It doesn't—they both have just seven.

BREAST CANCER AFFLICTS ONLY WOMEN

Though breast cancer is relatively rare in men, nearly 1,000 are diagnosed with the disease every year—about one for every 150 women who are afflicted—and nearly 300 die.

BROWN EGGS ARE MORE NUTRITIOUS THAN WHITE EGGS

The color of a fowl's eggshells is a protective camouflage against predators. Whether a chicken lays brown or white eggs is due to the geographic origin and survival requirements of its wild ancestors and does not affect the eggs' food value. According to a U.S. Department of Agriculture bulletin, "The eggs of any given breed of hens, whatever the color of the shells, are, on an average, as nutritious as those of any other breed, provided the eggs are of the same size and freshness and the fowls are equally well fed."

So where did this idea come from? Maybe the brown eggs look organic, while the white ones look like they've been put through some sort of nutrient-sapping bleaching process. Or it's just an association with other healthy foods, like brown bread and brown rice. If you shell out extra for the brown eggs, the yolk's on you.

A BULLET CAN KNOCK A MAN OVER; EXPLODE A GAS TANK

In the movies, a man struck by a bullet will usually be thrown back by the impact. This would violate Newton's third law of motion, which states that for every action, there is an equal and opposite

reaction. The actual force imparted by a bullet can be no greater than the force the shooter feels as recoil. A high-velocity bullet hitting a man in his chest creates an enormous shock to the nervous system, which may sometimes cause a muscular reaction, but any movement of this kind is muscular, not a reflection of the bullet's force. A dummy with the same resistance as a man will not move much when struck by a bullet. Captain F. E. Kleinschmidt, who filmed the Austrian army in action during World War I, observed that documentary footage often had to be faked or audiences wouldn't think it looked realistic. As he explained, "In real life a man who has been hit by a bullet does not throw up his hands and rifle and then fall in a theatrical fashion and roll a few times over. When he lies in the trenches and is hit he barely lurches a few inches forward or quietly turns on his side. The real picture is not as dramatic as the fake picture."

While we're at the movies, you may have noticed that when a bullet strikes the gas tank of a car (or any part of a car, if it's a Chuck Norris film), the vehicle instantly explodes in flames. This can happen, if gas leaks from the punctured tank onto a hot manifold, but a nonincendiary bullet fired into a gas tank will not by itself cause a fire. Tests have shown that an ordinary bullet fired through a gas tank will not cause a fire. A bullet does not heat up as it passes through the air, and so will not set anything ablaze. The SR-71 spy plane, after traveling several hours at Mach 3, got so hot it couldn't be touched for a considerable time after it landed, but that was a factor of its time in flight and the large mass of air it compressed ahead of it as it sped through the atmosphere. A bullet does not produce the same phenomenon—it is too small and travels for too short a period. When it flattens against a backstop it will heat up due to the energy released in deformation, but not while it's in flight.

BULLS HATE THE COLOR RED

In comedies and cartoons, wearing a red shirt in a bull's pasture is about as wise as flying a Confederate battle flag while driving through Detroit. The expression "like waving a red flag" has come to suggest provocation for that reason.

Bulls are not particularly enraged by the color red, as they are unable to distinguish any colors at all. When a matador waves a red cape, he is attempting to excite the crowd more than the bull—the bull responds solely to the cape's movement. Bulls are rather testy and it doesn't take much to annoy them. The matador could wave around a pink nightie or a tie-dyed T-shirt and get the same reaction.

BUMBLEBEES VIOLATE
THE LAWS OF AERODYNAMICS

In trying to illustrate the point that anything is possible, it is sometimes suggested that, after all, bumblebees violate every law of aerodynamics, yet still fly.

A bumblebee looks awkward when it flies, but it is certainly not violating any law of aerodynamics. You may be able to successfully violate one of Miss Manners' rules of etiquette, but when it comes to the laws of nature you have no choice but to obey.

The wings of a bumblebee look small in proportion to its body size when compared with those of a bird, but on the other hand, the rotors of a helicopter look small in comparison to the wings of an airplane. A bumblebee doesn't fly like an airplane, it flies like a helicopter.

BUNKER HILL IS THE SITE OF A FAMOUS BATTLE; IS WHERE THE ORDER "DON'T FIRE UNTIL YOU SEE THE WHITES OF THEIR EYES!" WAS FIRST ISSUED

The Battle of Bunker Hill was the first major engagement of the American Revolution, with a smaller force of colonials inflicting about 1,000 casualties on the British. The colonists were eventually driven off, but the number of British casualties made it a Pyrrhic victory for them. It was also a defeat for geography, as the battle was not fought on Bunker Hill but on nearby Breed's Hill. Rather than confuse people with the facts, Bostonians have simply renamed Breed's Hill Bunker Hill.

The event gave us one of our more memorable battle cries, Colonel William Prescott's order: "Don't fire until you see the whites of their eyes!" If he did say that, and there is no record that he did, he was not the first. A similar command was issued by Prince Charles of Prussia in 1745, and Frederick the Great in 1757. Several other commands that were tried proved unsuccessful. These included "Don't fire until you've counted the hairs in their nostrils" and "Don't fire until you can read the nametags in their undershorts."

CAGNEY SAID, "YOU DIRTY RAT!"

This line has been permanently grafted onto Jimmy Cagney by scores of impressionists, most notably Frank Gorshin, usually with a Cagneyesque "MMMMmmm" at the outset. Cagney never said the line, or anything even close, in any of the more than 70 movies he made.

CALL GIRLS ARE CALLED THAT BECAUSE YOU CALL THEM ON THE PHONE

The men's rooms of low-class bars are often decorated with women's names, telephone numbers and invitations to call, which would seem to suggest where the expression "call girl" comes from. In fact, the expression does not have anything to do with the use of the telephone to strike up an arrangement. It stems from the prostitute's association with what used to be called an assignation house, or "call house." The prostitute did not live at the house but would be called there as occasion arose by Miss Kitty, but not necessarily by Ma Bell.

CAMPUS REBELLION WAS FIRST SEEN IN THE SIXTIES

College offered a number of attractions in the 1960s. In addition to student draft deferments and free love, you might get your picture in *Life* magazine doing something glamorous like haranguing a crowd through a bullhorn or sitting with your feet up on the college president's desk, smoking his best cigars. The sixties was a decade of firsts, and among them seemed to be campus unrest.

According to historian Richard Shenkman, there had been any number of student rebellions throughout American history that were as turbulent as those of the sixties. In 1830 Yale experienced the "Conic Section's Rebellion," an uprising over a change in the teaching of mathematics, which resulted in the expulsion of 43 students, about half the class. In 1818 and 1828 there were student rebellions against the food, so serious that in both cases the campus had to be shut down. In the same period there was a window-smashing rampage at Christmas time; professors had to use fire axes to break down doors behind which students had locked themselves.

There were similar uprisings at other Ivy League schools in the early nineteenth century. Princeton had six such insurrections, and at Harvard several buildings were damaged with explosives. One Harvard spokesman commented that students were frequently "guilty of crimes worthy of the penitentiary." In 1836 soldiers had to be brought in to quell mob violence perpetrated by armed students at the University of Virginia.

Even the "silent generation"—students of the fifties—were not as law abiding as we imagine. Panty raids may seem like a tame joke now, but some of them involved thousands of male students on a rampage, tearing the clothes off of female students. At the University of California at Berkeley in 1956, one such "night of terror" resulted in several sexual assaults and $10,000 worth of property damage.

Local police had to help the campus cops restore order. A panty raid at the University of Ohio in 1958 got so wild that police had to use tear gas to drive the boys out of the girls' dorms.

CANARY ISLANDS WERE NAMED FOR CANARIES

The Canary Islands were not named for the little twittering birds that inhabited them—rather, it was the other way around. The Romans had already named the islands to the southwest of Spain for the wild dogs (*canes* in Latin) that roamed there; they were the Dog Islands, or *Canariae Insulae*. That makes the yellow songsters "dog" birds, if you think about it.

CAPE CANAVERAL IS THE LAUNCH PAD FOR SPACE MISSIONS

Florida's Cape Canaveral, called Cape Kennedy from 1963 through 1973, is known as the launching point for the Apollo expeditions and current space shuttle missions. In fact, the Kennedy Space Center from which the rockets depart lies on Merit Island, separated from the Cape by the Banana River. The last manned space flight from the Cape itself was over 30 years ago.

CAPTAIN BLIGH WAS THE VILLAIN OF THE *MUTINY ON THE BOUNTY*

If Captain Bligh knew that he would one day be tarred as one of history's great villains it would have come as a terrible shock to him. A ship's captain in 1789 did not tend to be the sensitive type, but as captains went, Bligh was not particularly harsh. He had seven men flogged during the voyage to Tahiti, but that was considered par for the course. Bligh was in fact unusually concerned with the well-being of his men, and when it was raining was known to give up his cabin so that wet sailors could dry off. He even brought a blind fiddler along on the *Bounty* to entertain the crew.

After the mutiny, half of the *Bounty*'s crew chose to stick with Bligh, though it meant being cast out to sea in an open boat with inadequate rations. Still, they fared better than the mutineers. In one of the greatest feats in seafaring history, Bligh navigated his boat 4,000 miles across the open Pacific to the island of Timor. In the course of this hellish journey, Bligh produced such excellent charts and descriptions of the waters that the Royal Navy relied upon them for decades

afterward. Bligh received a hero's welcome back in England, and eventually retired with the rank of Vice Admiral of the Blue. As for the mutineers, some were captured on Tahiti and either died en route back to England or were hanged when they got there. Those who fled to Pitcairn Island were mostly killed off, by each other or by their lovely and uninhibited Polynesian wives. Decades later the Royal Navy arrived at Pitcairn and found John Adams, the sole survivor.

Why has Bligh gotten such a black eye? To make a good melodrama you need a villain, and for modern audiences the story works best as a tale of rebellion against a harsh authority, of shucking the restraints of a constraining social order in pursuit of paradise.

CAPTAIN KIRK SAID, "BEAM ME UP, SCOTTY"

Trekkies, who know everything from Romulan curses to Spock's shoe size, report that Captain Kirk never uttered this immortal line on *Star Trek*. What he usually said was "Beam us up, Mr. Scott" or "Enterprise, beam us up." On the fourth episode, Kirk actually does say, "Scotty, beam me up" but only once, and that was as close as he got.

CAPTAIN OF THE SHIP CAN PERFORM WEDDINGS

At the end of *African Queen*, Bogart and Hepburn are married by the captain of a ship that rescued them, so they can enjoy conjugal bliss until their obvious and complete incompatibility catches up with them in a week or so. Adding spice to the relationship is the fact that they wouldn't actually be legally married. The captain of a ship has no particular power to perform weddings, as was established in an 1898 case, *Norman v. Norman*. Regulations in the U.S., British and Soviet navies, as well as those of other nations, specifically prohibit a commanding officer from performing marriage ceremonies. The belief that the captain has such authority is probably based on the almost total power he exercises while at sea.

CARBURETORS EXIST THAT WOULD GIVE YOUR CAR 200 MPG

This is one of the rumors that circulates among the mildly paranoid. You see, someone has invented a carburetor that is so efficient that it would enable your car to get 200 mpg, but Big Oil and the automakers have suppressed it. People who believe this will also tell you about the tires that last indefinitely (Big Rubber's sitting on that one), the cure for cancer the American Medical Association doesn't want you to have, and the Illuminati who actually choose our presidents (nice to think we could be off the hook).

Charles N. Pogue is supposed to have invented such a device in the mid-1930s. By preheating the gasoline it vaporized it more thoroughly, enabling the engine to use the fuel more efficiently. Similar high-mileage "vapor" carburetors are still hustled to the gullible today, but those who offer them through the mail claiming anything like 200 mpg can be prosecuted for mail fraud.

An ordinary car burns gasoline fairly well as is—97% of the fuel combusts. The fact that the engine transforms only 35% of the gasoline's energy to power is not the fault of the carburetor; when it comes to fuel efficiency, it makes a fairly small contribution. Much more mileage can be squeezed from improved aerodynamics, greater use of lightweight materials, better tires, advanced transmissions and other innovations. Unfortunately, maximum fuel efficiency comes at a cost—either cars would become more expensive to produce or so small and lightweight that they would be dangerous in an accident and offer inadequate power and passenger room.

As long as gas remains reasonably cheap, the public is not particularly interested in either course.

CARROTS WILL IMPROVE YOUR VISION

Carrots are good sources of carotene, which the body transforms into vitamin A. The body uses vitamin A to produce the retinal pigment rhodopsin; without it, a person would suffer from night blindness. Many people, including scientists in the past, have therefore assumed that eating carrots is important for good vision. (As the joke goes, have you ever seen a rabbit wearing glasses?) However, most people get all the vitamin A they can use by eating normally, and the liver stores plenty in case of any shortfall. Excess amounts of the vitamin cannot be used by the body and don't lead to any heightened visual acuity. During World War II, pilots were given large doses of vitamin A in hopes that it would improve their vision, but tests found it made no perceptible difference.

CATHERINE THE GREAT DIED
TRYING TO HAVE SEX WITH A HORSE

Catherine the Great, empress from 1762 to 1796, was one of Russia's most famous rulers. Interestingly, she herself wasn't Russian but German, and her real name was Sophia. She was considered an "enlightened despot," which is about as good as it got in those days.

The story, passed around by generations of in-the-know college freshmen, is that she was sexually insatiable. No man could satisfy her—she needed a *real* stud. While a horse was being lowered upon her through some sort of pulley arrangement, the attendants lost their grip on the ropes and the horse crushed her. Hot stuff.

Catherine the Great *did* work her way through a number of two-legged lovers, probably a dozen or so. Her enemies sought to undercut her authority by exaggerating her licentiousness, and they're probably the ones who hitched her up with Mr. Ed. The truth is that the empress died of a stroke at age 67, falling from the commode in her personal quarters at the St. Petersburg palace. There was no horseplay involved.

CATS ARE THE SOURCE OF CATGUT

Catgut has been used for centuries to string musical instruments, but cat lovers need not cry for all the lap-loungers that gave their lives that a violin might live. *Catgut* is a term for a tough cord made from chemically treated animal intestines, but the animals who supplied it have always been sheep, not cats. Cat intestines would not make a particularly good catgut. The association is understandable, though: Listen to kids practicing their violins, then to a cat whose tail is caught under a rocking chair.

CHIEF SEATTLE MADE AN ELOQUENT STATEMENT ON ECOLOGY

Chief Seattle, of the Suquamish and Dowamish tribes, when forced to sell tribal lands in the mid-nineteenth century, is quoted as having made a lengthy, eloquent statement beginning with the words:

"How can you buy the sky? How can you own the rain and the wind? My mother told me, every part of this earth is sacred to my people. Every pine needle. Every sandy shore. Every mist in the dark woods. Every meadow and humming insect. All are holy in the memory of our people."

The statement went on in the same elegant simplicity, a moving expression of the Indians' reverence for the land. It appeared on posters, in speeches and in writings on the environment. Mythologist Joseph Campbell quoted it at length during his televised interviews with PBS' Bill Moyers, and Moyers included it in his book *The Power of Myth*. It inspired one of 1991's best-selling children's books, *Brother Eagle, Sister Sky: A Message from Chief Seattle*. Clearly, it speaks to our times and to our own concerns for the future of our planet.

The only problem is that Chief Seattle never said it. The statement was written by screenwriter Ted Perry for a 1972 documentary on the environment. His research failed to turn up any record of a Native American speech extolling the sanctity of the earth, so he wrote one himself and put it into the chief's mouth, using a few of the chief's own words. Only when the film had been finished did Perry discover that credit for the words had been given to Chief Seattle. When Perry complained, the producers explained that doing it this way added "authenticity." Why settle for the truth when you can have authenticity?

CHRISTMAS IS THE BIRTHDAY OF CHRIST

When recounting the story of Jesus' birth, ministers will often remind their flocks that even in the Middle East, late December is a chilly time of the year to be born in a stable. That poignant detail is somewhat deflated by the fact that no one knows for certain on what day of the year Jesus Christ was born. At that time birth dates—even the birth dates of notable people—were not considered particularly significant; the dates of their deaths were of greater import. The question of Jesus' precise birthday never even came up until the third century A.D., when Clement of Alexandria suggested May 20. In 336 the Church of Rome settled on December 25, while the Eastern Church picked January 6, which in the Armenian Church is still celebrated as Christmas Day. The reason for the choice was the church's desire to absorb pagan holidays held around the winter solstice. Christianity had probably the best marketing strategy of any major religion, and this approach was sheer genius. The December 25 Roman holiday of Natalis Solis Invicti, the Birthday of the Unconquerable Sun, thus segued neatly into the Christian holiday. Other pagan customs, such as the tree worship of the druids and primitive Scandinavians, were also accommodated.

Historians and theologians consider it unlikely that there is even a 1-in-365 chance that Christ's birthday falls on December 25. The shepherds mentioned in the Biblical account would probably not have been out at that time of the year. October or November have been pegged as more likely, and some argue for a date as early as July. This would have been a better deal for Jesus—as we know, if your birthday falls on December 25, you don't end up getting your fair share of presents.

Speaking of birthday presents, Jesus was supposed to have received some from three wise men, sometimes referred to as three kings. Nothing in the Gospels suggests that they were kings; they were probably astrologers. The Gospels also never mention that there were three of them. The number is extrapolated from Matthew's reference to the three gifts they brought: gold, frankincense and myrrh. Myrrh is a bitter, reddish brown gum resin; what Jesus was supposed to do with it is one of those ecclesiastical mysteries we were probably never meant to understand. George Carlin speculates that Jesus would rather have had the money, so he could have bought something he really wanted.

CHURCHILL BROADCAST A SPEECH IN WHICH HE OFFERED THE BRITISH NOTHING BUT "BLOOD, SWEAT AND TEARS"

Before Blood, Sweat, and Tears was a rock group it was a phrase attributed to Winston Churchill. In fact, though, those were not the words he used in his famous 1940 speech. As to what the English could expect from the war with Germany, Churchill had said, "I have nothing to offer but blood, toil, tears and sweat." The phrase was edited and rearranged in the minds of his audience to produce a smoother flow. It works better with the list restricted to bodily fluids, and "toil" seems redundant when sweat is mentioned.

The version of this speech that was broadcast over the radio and that is still heard on World War II documentaries was not delivered by Churchill himself, but by an actor. Churchill had delivered the speech, his first as prime minister, before the House of Parliament, but it had not been recorded. Since he had a rather pressing schedule, what with trying to form a new government while the Nazis were speedily conquering Europe, a character actor was found whose Churchill impression was good enough to fill in.

CIA AGENTS ARE GLOBE-TROTTING ADVENTURERS

Most of us have probably fantasized about being a CIA agent, traveling around the world making interesting mischief with our nifty

little guns and gadgets. No doubt most of the people who work for the CIA fantasize about the same thing—less than 5% of them are involved in what we would consider spying or covert operations. The rest are technicians and academics (in Company lingo, "nerds and buffs") who spend their lives analyzing brain-numbing trivia. About half of the intelligence information the CIA gathers is from satellite photography and imaging, as well as electronic data gathering. Dealing with this stuff is the duty of the nerds. The buffs are the experts in various arcane academic disciplines. The CIA hires more Ph.D.s than any other government agency; it's one of the few places you can get a job if you wrote a doctoral thesis on Siberian geography, Indonesian dialects, undersea topography or microwave propagation. You know the type—they couldn't get a date for the senior prom.

Is a spy's life this glamorous?

CLEOPATRA WAS EGYPTIAN, ETC.

There is a lot of talk lately suggesting that the ancient Egyptians were black, which comes as something of a surprise to present day residents

of the region. When it comes to Egypt's most famous queen, Cleopatra, it should be noted that not only was she not black, she was not even Egyptian, but rather part Greek, part Macedonian and part Iranian.

There were actually seven queens named Cleopatra, and the one that Elizabeth Taylor played was properly known as Cleopatra VII Thea Philopator. She was the last of the Ptolemaic dynasty that ruled Egypt for 250 years until it was annexed by the Romans in 31 B.C. Cleopatra ruled from Alexandria, which, except for its location, was not an Egyptian city at all. Greek was the language of the court, and Cleopatra was the only one in her family who bothered to learn the Egyptian language. If she ever wore Egyptian costume, it was only on ceremonial occasions.

Several other myths about her remain:
—Realistic portraits of her indicate that she was no one's idea of a fabulous babe. She got her way through her charm and intelligence, not her looks.
—As an example of her decadence, it is said that she dissolved a large pearl in a cup of vinegar and drank it. But she couldn't have, since pearls don't dissolve in vinegar, now or then.
—Claudette Colbert and Elizabeth Taylor both played her in bangs, but that was merely the fashion when the films were made. In keeping with the fashion of her own time, Cleopatra wore a wig of tight curls over a shaved head.

—There's no proof that she killed herself by clasping an asp to her bosom, though it would have been fitting—the asp was the symbol of Egyptian royalty. She probably killed herself not out of grief for Antony, but from dread that she would be taken prisoner and paraded through Rome in chains. Humiliation was not entirely averted, however. Rumor has it that Cleopatra's mummified remains, looted from Egypt by Napoleon, were inadvertently dumped into the Paris sewers by workmen in the 1940s.

CLOCKS ON DISPLAY ARE SET AT 8:20 TO MARK THE TIME OF LINCOLN'S DEATH

The clocks shown in catalogs are generally set at 8:20. Somewhere along the line an inquiring mind asked why, and someone ingeniously explained that it's because that was the time that Lincoln died. The story seems to have stuck.

Lincoln is known to have died at 7:30 A.M. The reason that display clocks are usually set at 8:20 (or more precisely, 8:18) is that it looks nice—symmetrical and relaxed. The manufacturer's name, usually on the vertical axis, is clearly exposed with room for additional advertising.

COBRAS CAN BE HYPNOTIZED BY THE MUSIC OF SNAKE CHARMERS

The image of the cobra rising from its basket and swaying to the music of the snake charmer's flute is a familiar one. Though the idea of a deadly snake being hypnotized by music is compelling, the cobra, like all snakes, is deaf. It is able to detect vibration, but it cannot hear. The cobra is responding to the movement of the flute, rather than its sound, and far from being charmed it is trying to position itself to strike. The snake charmer stays out of striking range and, if he needs an extra dollop of confidence, removes his pet's fangs or sews its mouth shut.

COCA-COLA WILL DISSOLVE A TOOTH PUT IN IT OVERNIGHT; THE COMBINATION OF COKE AND AN ASPIRIN WILL GET YOU HIGH

Teeth regularly bathed in Coca-Cola stand a good chance of developing tooth decay, but there is no truth to the belief that a tooth dropped into a glass of Coca-Cola will dissolve overnight. In *Myth-Informed*, authors Paul Dickson and Joseph C. Goulden mention a friend who has kept a tooth in a regularly-replenished glass of Coke for over ten years as an ongoing study. It has developed "a lovely patina" but has so far survived intact.

The rumor that drinking Coca-Cola in combination with a few aspirin will get you high has even less foundation in truth.

COLD WEATHER CAUSES COLDS

Even in this enlightened age, one cannot go out lightly dressed in cold weather without being warned about the risk of catching a cold. In fact, cold weather and colds have very little to do with each other. The only way to pick up a cold is to catch the latest mutation of the diabolical rhinovirus that's going around. Polar explorers have noted that even after weeks of struggling through the blowing snow and frigid temperatures, suffering from exhaustion, exposure and undernourishment, they did not catch colds until they returned to civilization.

Isn't it true that a chill can lower our resistance to infection, making us more likely to succumb to a virus that we might otherwise have fought off? Sounds plausible, but even this theory hasn't proven itself in tests. Researchers have exposed volunteers to the cold virus, then subjected a test sample of them to a variety of temperature conditions. (You have to wonder who volunteers for these things.) Some sat around in their underwear in 40°F temperatures, others were immersed in cool water to bring their body temperature down. These tests were done throughout the whole life of the disease, from initial infection to the recovery stage. The cold temperatures made no apparent difference in the number or severity of colds that developed between the sample that was subjected to this abuse and the control group.

Cold season does seem to coincide with cold weather. Scientists speculate that the cold weather forces people indoors, where they are in greater proximity to each other. The dry air in winter, both indoors and out, dries the mucous membranes inside the nose, hampering their protective function. Children are in schools and day care, where viruses are more readily passed around to each other and then to their parents. Schools and daycare centers make such suitable breeding grounds for germs that pediatricians call them "culture" centers.

COLONIAL AMERICANS WERE SEXUALLY REPRESSED

Sex isn't something that came in with rock and roll. Although there is more sexual openness now than in the past, our forefathers were not as uptight as most people imagine. In Bristol, Rhode Island, in a 20-year period in the late 1700s, nearly half of all newlywed couples had a baby before they had been married nine months. During the same period in Concord, Massachusetts, a third of all the babies were conceived out of wedlock. In addition, we have to assume that there was plenty of premarital sex going on that didn't result in pregnancy.

The Puritans have been singled out as the source of a residual American discomfort with sex, but even their propriety is overstated. Parents and children usually lived in the same room, and there's just so much you can keep under wraps. While Puritans believed in chastity, they considered sex within marriage a very good thing and talked about the matter openly. When it came out that a member of the First Church of Boston had refused to sleep with his wife for two years, the matter was discussed by the congregation, which decided to expel him.

One of the more surprising rituals of courtship among early New Englanders was the practice of "bundling." Teenaged girls were permitted to sleep in the same bed with their boyfriends, as long as both remained clothed and had, as one commentator put it, "the shared understanding that innocent endearments should not be exceeded." Sometimes a board was placed between them, and there were special chastity-protecting garments for the girls. Anyone who's ever been a teenager can imagine how successful these precautions were, and many little bundles of joy were the product of bundling. One song of the period told of the "bundling maid" who would "sometimes say when she lies down/ She can't be cumbered with a gown."

COLUMBUS PROVED THE WORLD WAS ROUND; DISCOVERED AMERICA; ETC.

We're taught a lot of egregious nonsense in grade school (in college too, come to think of it) and sometimes it's hard to sort it all out.

Most of us have labored under the impression that one of Columbus' challenges was to convince his contemporaries that the world is round, and that it was possible to reach the Indies by sailing west. According to the story, not only were the backers dubious, but his sailors were terrified that they would disappear over the earth's edge. This version of history was contained in a biography of Columbus by Washington Irving, of *Rip van Winkle* fame. In fact, few Europeans in the fifteenth century still believed the earth was flat. As early as the sixth century B.C., Pythagoras put forth the view that the earth was a globe. The second-century Alexandrian astronomer and geographer Ptolemy agreed, on the basis that the shadow the earth cast on the moon during an eclipse was round. He also believed that the eastern end of the Eurasian land mass could be reached by sailing west. Columbus owned and studied the 1480 edition of *Imago Mundi* ("Image of the World") by Pierre D'Ailly, which calculated that the Atlantic was less wide than had been believed. Columbus' great innovation was to so seriously underestimate the width of the ocean that he could persuasively argue that he could sail across it. The actual distance from the Canary Islands to Japan is 10,000 miles; Columbus figured it to be about 2,400 and got backing on that basis. Fortunately, 2,400 miles got him to the Americas, and if they hadn't happened to have been there he would have really been up the creek.

Columbus gets credit for discovering America, despite the fact that he never actually set foot on the North American mainland. His initial discovery was of Watlings Island in the Bahamas. In his three subsequent excursions across the Atlantic, his landings were all in the Caribbean and South America. It was Juan Ponce de León who finally set foot on Florida in 1513. Columbus, convinced he had reached India, never claimed to have discovered the New World.

Christopher Columbus wouldn't have been able to cash a check written out to that name. It's an Anglicized version of his original Italian name, Cristforo Colombo. However, Columbus left his native country before he could write, and when he did learn, it was in Spain. Throughout his life he signed his name Cristóbal Colón, a Castilian translation, and it was that name by which he was known.

Despite various artistic conceptions of Columbus, we have no real idea what he looked like beyond a description supplied by his son. There were no portraits painted of him during his lifetime.

Those who want to split hairs may point out that Columbus

couldn't have proved the world round because it is not round. The earth is an oblate sphere, 13 miles greater in diameter at the equator than at the poles.

COMBAT IS THE LEADING CAUSE OF DEATH IN WAR

Throughout history more soldiers have died from disease than from enemy action, and it is only recently, with the advent of antibiotics,

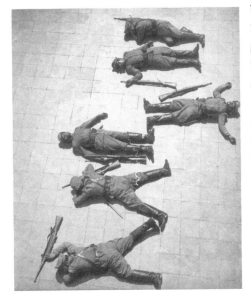

that this has ceased to be true. The introduction in World War I of such efficient killers as poison gas, machine guns and tanks did not change the equation—disease, particularly influenza, accounted for almost 63,000 out of America's 113,000 deaths. Even in World War II it is estimated that almost half of all deaths, civilian and military, were due to disease. Typhus was one of the deadliest killers. Due to the typhus-carrying lice that infested Russian troops, Germans in World War I used to joke that it was more dangerous to shake hands with a Russian than to be shot at by him. Outbreaks were particularly lethal in POW and concentration camps; it was typhus that killed Anne Frank at Bergen-Belsen a few weeks before the end of World War II. Malaria

was a particular problem for those fighting in the Pacific, most of whom were from nontropical areas and had no immunity to the disease. As many American troops were put out of action by malaria as by the enemy.

COMETS ARE BALLS OF
FIRE STREAKING THROUGH SPACE

As long as more people get their information about the universe from *Star Wars* than from public television's *Nova*, the comet will continue to be depicted as a fireball streaking through space trailing flames. According to astronomers, though, it's more like a "dirty snowball" consisting of a nucleus of frozen gases and dust that, when heated by the Sun, produces a large cloud or "coma" which surrounds the core. The tail is composed of gas and dust particles pushed out by the pressure of sunlight photons. A comet gives off no light, but merely reflects that of the sun.

CONDEMNED MURDERERS ARE FREED IF MECHANICAL FAILURE PREVENTS THEIR EXECUTION

After someone's taken that long drop on a short rope only to have the rope break, it seems fair that he should be given a pass. Even fans of capital punishment might accept the argument that, hey, he got the point. Besides, it could be the Hand of God at work, and you don't want to mess with that. Nevertheless, there is nothing in English or American law that suggests that the condemned party should be freed if the execution fails. People confuse the situation with protection against double jeopardy, which means that no one can be tried twice for the same crime. Once the miscreant's been tried and convicted, the authorities can keep trying to kill him until they get it right.

THE CONSTITUTION INCLUDES A WALL OF SEPARATION BETWEEN CHURCH AND STATE

In any debate over school vouchers for parochial schools, nativity scenes of the courthouse lawn, prayer in the schools, etc., "the wall of separation between church and state" is bound to be brought up. Many people assume that this phrase is part of the Constitution; in fact, the phrase occurs nowhere in the 7,544 words of the Constitution or its 27 amendments, nor does the word *separation* nor the word *church*. The First Amendment of the Bill of Rights addresses religion only to this extent: "Congress shall make no law respecting an establishment of religion, or prohibiting the free exercise thereof."

Though the phrase is not in the Constitution, it was coined by the main author of that document, Thomas Jefferson. More than any of the other Founding Fathers, he believed in "the wall of separation between church and state" as we understand it today. Jefferson first used the expression in a letter to a committee of Baptists in Connecticut in 1802, while he was President of the United States. He wrote:

Believing with you that religion is a matter which lies solely between man and his God, that he owes account to none other for his faith or his worship, that the legislative powers of government reach actions only, and not opinions, I contemplate with sovereign reverence that act of the whole American people which declared that their legislature should make no law respecting an establishment of religion, or prohibiting the free exercise thereof, thus building *a wall of separation between Church and State* [emphasis added].

The phrase became a favorite of Supreme Court justices in the 1960s.

CONTORTIONISTS ARE DOUBLE JOINTED

Stage contortionists and yoga adepts are capable of tying themselves into such knots that they're described as "double jointed." There's no such thing as a double joint, though. Extreme flexibility is developed through constant stretching of muscles and ligaments.

CORINTHIAN LEATHER

No one who ever heard Ricardo Montalban pitching the 1974 Chrysler Cordoba can forget the car's most desirable feature—the one that Montalban singled out for effusive praise. It was, of course, the "reech Co-REEN-thee-an leather" that upholstered the car's seats. He almost salivated as he described it.

The *Wall Street Journal* decided to look into this fabled old-world product and revealed in an article titled "Department of Shattered Illusions" that "Corinthian leather" was just a marketing name applied to leather tanned to Chrysler's specifications. It did not come from Greece, site of the ancient city of Corinth, but from processors in Newark, New Jersey, and other American sources. ("Reech New JER-sey-an leather" doesn't roll off the tongue quite as smoothly.)

Montalban described Corinthian leather as "the best," but few agreed. *Consumer Reports* said the material "doesn't feel that terrific."

COUPONS—YOU SAVE MONEY BY USING THEM

Every once in a while a story will appear in a tabloid magazine about some master shopper who bought $116.94 worth of groceries for $23.39 using coupons. The implication is that if you do not conscientiously clip, file and use those little chits you're just throwing money away.

The truth is somewhat different. Coupons are usually for national brands, and coupon shoppers may tend to overlook equally good alternative brands that cost less than the name item with or without the discount. Industry studies have shown that frequent coupon users tend to have higher grocery bills than those who shop without them—as much as 84% higher. They buy higher-priced goods and make more impulse purchases.

Manufacturers offer coupons for promotional purposes, not so that the consumer can save money. The cost of the coupons—advertising, processing and redemption value—is added on to the cost of the product. An additional cost is the fraudulent use of coupons by unscrupulous store owners and clerks. Although only five out of 100 coupons are ever redeemed, the industry estimates that one of those five is redeemed by someone not entitled to the money. We pay for that too, as you may have guessed.

CRUDE OIL IS ALWAYS BLACK; GUSHES FROM WELLS

Most of us who have seen *The Beverly Hillbillies* know what oil looks like when it comes out of the ground. "Black gold" as the theme song called it, as black as what we drain from our crankcase.

Actually, crude oil is usually, but not always black—it can also be brown, red, amber, green or nearly colorless. The color varies from place to place, depending on the particular mixture of hydrocarbons involved. Oil is not necessarily liquid, either—it can be as thick as peanut butter.

Oil no longer gushes orgasmically out of wells when a strike is made. Since the 1930s, drilling crews have used blowout preventers to stop gushers. A gusher is an unlikely and unwelcome accident.

Most of us think of oil deposits as the remains of primeval forests, with a few *Velociraptors* tossed in for that high-octane kick. Scientists now believe that they were formed from the remains of tiny aquatic plants and animals that lived in ancient seas. When they died they sank to the bottom and, over millions of years, were transformed through a process too uninteresting to describe into crude oil and natural gas.

THE DARK AGES WERE A DARK TIME FOR HUMANITY

The Dark Ages, between the Fall of the Roman Empire and the Renaissance, get a bad rap, as if everything was covered in gloom.

What exactly was so dark about them?

A lot of people lived as serfs, but that was actually a step in the right direction. Slavery ended in Europe with the fall of Rome, along with crucifixion and those sold-out shows in which people were fed to wild animals. Christianity thrived. Gothic architecture was invented, and the Notre-Dame de Paris and Chartres were built. Oxford University began accepting students. Aristotle was rediscovered and experimental science began. The tenth century saw the invention of the rigid horse collar, which revolutionized agriculture.

What about all the superstition? And witch burning? Superstition was more prevalent under the pagan Romans—the Catholic Church frowned on that sort of thing. People in the Dark Ages may have believed in witches, but they rarely burned them. That started after the Renaissance.

So why did the Dark Ages get such a dreary image? Largely due to the prodigious PR machine of the Renaissance. It made itself look good by making what preceded it look really awful. It was in the Renaissance that the glorious architecture of the Middle Ages was termed *Gothic*—Renaissance snobs thought it was so ugly and barbarous that it should be named after the Goths.

DARK SIDE OF THE MOON

Though we sometimes speak of the dark side of the moon, there is no such thing. Every last acre of the moon is illuminated at some point during the month-long lunar cycle. Because the same side of the moon always faces the earth, there is a side of the moon that we never see, but it's not always dark. It is illuminated during the new moon phase.

DARWIN CLAIMED THAT
MAN EVOLVED FROM THE APES

Leading skeptics to wonder—why don't apes continue to evolve into people?

Actually, the theory of evolution propounded by Charles Darwin does not claim that man evolved from apes, or even vice versa. It claims that man and the apes evolved from the a common ancestor. Scientists believe that the split occurred about 5 million years ago.

It should also be noted that Darwin did not invent the theory of evolution. The idea that species change over time had previously been proposed by the Greek philosophers Anaximander and Empedocles; the Enlightenment thinkers Newton, Leibniz and de Maillet; and naturalists Georges Buffon and Carolus Linnaeus. Even Darwin's grandfather had published a book suggesting that the animal world might have "arisen from one filament" with the capability of "continuing to improve by its own inherent activity, and of delivering down those improvements by generation to its posterity." The year before Darwin published his *Origin of Species*, he read a paper by English naturalist Alfred Russel Wallace that outlined a theory of evolution remarkably like Darwin's own, including the insight most identified with Darwin, the process of natural selection. (To his credit, Darwin acknowledged Wallace's

work.) Darwin's great contribution to evolutionary theory was the massive body of evidence he assembled to support it.

Darwin also did not coin the phrase "survival of the fittest." That was offered by the philosopher Herbert Spencer, who did much to popularize the theory.

THE DEATH PENALTY KILLS

You can debate whether or not the death penalty is a deterrent, but surely everyone would agree that being sentenced to death would tend to shorten your life. Columnist Steven Chapman offers the intriguing argument that when you sentence someone to death, you are probably *extending* his or her life. After all, very few residents on death row actually get executed every year; last year only 31 from a population of around 3,000 were done in. Those arriving on death row are increasingly likely to have been employed in the violence-prone drug business. While no one has figured out exactly what the death rate is for people trafficking in hard drugs, it is bound to be a lot higher than the 1% on death row who are legally executed each year. Chapman quotes Professor Arthur Alschuler of the University of Chicago law school as guessing that a drug dealer on death row has a longer life expectancy than one on the street.

While on the subject, it should be noted that contrary to what you see in the movies, the lights in the prison do not dim when

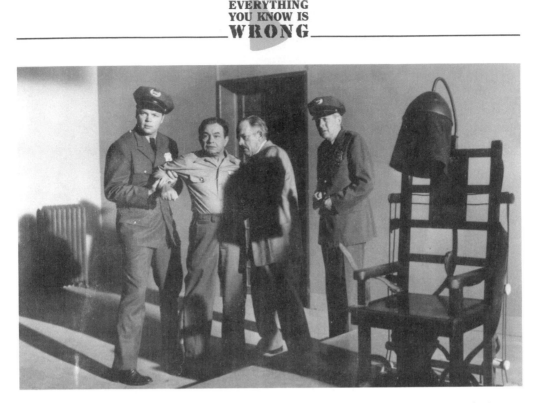

they throw the switch for the electric chair. The electric chair creates a short circuit in the body of the condemned and, for that reason, cannot be part of the prison's regular electrical system. It requires its own separate power supply.

THE DECLARATION OF INDEPENDENCE WAS SIGNED BY ALL THE FRAMERS ON JULY 4, 1776

Why is the Fourth of July a national holiday? Because it is the date that all the Framers got together and signed the Declaration of Independence, most of us would answer—wrongly.

The motion for a declaration of independence was originally introduced by Richard Henry Lee of Virginia on June 7, 1776. A committee was formed to draw up the document. Thomas Jefferson wrote it, revisions were supplied by Benjamin Franklin and John Adams and further revisions were made when it was submitted to the Continental Congress.

On July 2, 1776, the Congress approved a resolution formally cutting America's ties with England and expressing our intention to become independent. That night the Pennsylvania *Evening Post* was headlined: "This day the Continental Congress declared the United Colonies Free and Independent States." John Adams thought that date would be one that would live on. As he wrote in a letter to his wife: "The Second Day of July...ought to be commemorated...It ought to be solemnized with pomp and parade, with shows, games, sports, guns, bells, bonfires, and illuminations—from this time forward for everyone." (When a nineteenth-century scholar came across this letter, he simply altered the dates to conform to the accepted dates.)

On July 4, 1776, Jefferson completed his first draft of the Declaration, describing the theory behind our government and listing the grievances we had against England. The draft was accepted by the Continental Congress and on that day was signed only by John Hancock and Charles Thomson. The draft then went to the printer. It carries the date we all remember.

On July 8 the Congress celebrated independence with the firing of guns and a parade. Washington's army in New York got the word July 9. Celebrations were held in other colonies when they got the news some time later.

By August 2, 1776, the final parchment copy was ready and 50 assembled delegates signed it. Others signed months later, and Thomas McLean didn't get his name on it until 1781.

Our confusion is understandable, in that both Benjamin Franklin and Thomas Jefferson were under the impression that the Declaration had been signed by all the Framers on July 4 rather than August 2. It's just as well. If Independence Day was that close to Labor Day, it would make the summer seem entirely too short.

DIAMONDS ARE THE MOST VALUABLE GEM DUE TO THEIR RARITY

The ruby, not the diamond, is the most valuable gem. A 10-carat top-quality ruby can sell for more than $200,000 a carat, four times the price of a flawless white diamond of the same size. The diamond is also not terribly rare; in fact, it is the world's most common gem. However, it is prized for its beauty and is expensive to cut and polish because of its hardness. It has numerous critical industrial and scientific applications as well. Mostly though, its value is artificially maintained by the Central Selling Organization (CSO), which takes its orders from De Beers Consolidated Mines, Ltd., the giant South African mining operation. De Beers and its affiliates produce about half the world's diamonds, and CSO buys up about half of the remaining supply, enabling it to control the flow of three-quarters of all the diamonds that reach the market. It is De Beers that sponsors those "diamonds are forever" commercials that have effectively convinced consumers that the diamond is the most desirable jewel. If it weren't for this promotion and price fixing, who knows what a diamond would actually sell for?

Though we think of diamonds as clear and colorless, they may be translucent or even opaque and come in a range of colors. The clear, gem-quality stone is the most valuable, along with other colored tints such as blue, green, yellow, orange and red. Clouded or opaque stones and those in darker colors such as gray, brown or black are less valuable and are used for industrial purposes.

DINOSAURS FAILED AS A SPECIES; WERE GIANT LIZARDS; WERE THE LARGEST ANIMALS ON EARTH

Polls show that an alarming percentage of Americans believe that dinosaurs existed at the same time as early man. Apparently, when it comes to molding public opinion, hard science is no match for the *Flintstones* and *One Million Years, B.C.* At the same time, no film featuring people and dinosaurs includes the primitive mammals that actually *did* live alongside dinosaurs—animals that predated the arrival of mankind by over a hundred million years. It should also be noted that many of the primitive reptiles we imagine living side by side

Enduring misinformation from *One Million Years B.C.*

did not occupy the planet within eons of each other. The *Dimetrodon*, that lizard-looking thing with the great sailfin on its back, flourished at the end of the Paleozoic era, a geologic era that preceded the arrival of the dinosaurs. The *Dimetrodon* was a mammal-like reptile, part of the group from which evolved both dinosaurs and mammals, and had less in common with them than it did with us.

Paleontologists bristle when they hear some short-lived commercial failure disparagingly called "a dinosaur." They are quick to point out that dinosaurs, far from being a failure, were an astonishingly successful life-form, dominating the earth for 160 million years. Mammals lived alongside them for most of that time and were not able to successfully compete, never evolving above the level of primitive shrews and hedgehogs. It was only with the passing of the dinosaurs, for whatever reason, that mammals were able to finally come into their own. So let's not get uppity. Modern man has been here for less than 50,000, and look at the mess we've made of things.

Though their name means "monstrous lizards," dinosaurs had nothing in common with lizards of today. Their skeletal system was different than any known reptile, with legs that extended straight down rather than to the sides, enabling them to walk like mammals. They also weren't all large and lumbering—there were dinosaurs no bigger than chickens.

When conversing with any dinosaur expert, and that may include your six-year-old nephew, don't identify anything as a *Brontosaurus*. What we used to call a *Brontosaurus* we now call an *Apatosaurus*. In the 1870s, when paleontologists were digging up bones right and left and slapping names on any skeleton they could cobble together, things got confused. The name *Brontosaurus* ("thunder lizard") was misapplied to a species that had been identified several years earlier as the *Apatosaurus* ("deceptive lizard"). You'd have to say *Brontosaurus* is the better name, since it's one of the few that everyone knows. But scientific rules are clear—the first name given to a species is the correct one.

Though dinosaurs got pretty large, they were not the largest animals that have ever lived. The blue whale can reach 110 feet in length and can weigh up to 175 tons, nearly three times the weight of a *Brachiosaurus*.

DOCK, PIER AND WHARF
ALL MEAN THE SAME THING

When Otis Redding sang soulfully about "Sitting on the Dock on the Bay," he was using the word *dock* the way most of us do—incorrectly. If he meant one of those wooden structures jutting out onto the water on pilings, he should have said a *pier* or a *wharf*. If he really sat on a dock he would have had good reason to sing the blues, since he would have gotten soaked. In proper nautical terminology, a dock is the area of water that a ship parks, or "docks," in. It's generally next to a pier or wharf, the platform to which the ship can be moored and from which it is loaded and unloaded.

A pier and a wharf are not exactly the same either: A pier sticks out into the water, usually perpendicular to the shore, while a wharf runs parallel to the shoreline.

DOG DAYS OF SUMMER ARE NAMED AFTER DOGS

The image would seem to be self-explanatory...Ole Beauregard flopped out on the verandah, pressed into immobility by the sheer weight of the summer swelter, tongue lolling out, barely twitching at the flies...Only, in fact, the expression "dog days" has nothing to do with overheated hounds. Around 2770 B.C., the Romans observed that the brightest star in the sky, Sirius (AKA Alpha Canis Majoris, AKA the Dog Star) rose in conjunction with the sun for a 40-day period from early July until the middle of August. They theorized that the attendant heat was due to the combination of our sun augmented by the power of Sirius. This gave us the expression "the dog days of summer" for that period, which is the hottest of the year.

What with leap years adding a day every four-year cycle, the astronomical event no longer necessarily coincides with the summer months. However, the expression has stuck, and will as long as local TV stations can illustrate a summer story with footage of a panting pooch.

A DOG'S NOSE SHOULD BE
COLD AND WET OR ELSE IT'S SICK

Many pet owners think that a dog with a hot, dry nose must necessarily be sick. In fact, it usually only means that the dog has been inactive for a while, sleeping or resting—in other words, doing its job.

A DOG YEAR IS EQUAL TO SEVEN HUMAN YEARS

"My dog's three years old—but that's twenty-one in people years."

The idea that a year in the life of a dog is the equivalent of seven in the life of a human shouldn't survive a momentary exertion of logic. Dogs mature much more quickly than humans in the first year of their lives. A six-month-old puppy has nearly reached its adult size, and a one-year-old dog can produce puppies. Furthermore, dogs have lived as long as 34 years—that's 238 in people years!

A more sensible rule for figuring the equivalency of a dog's age is 15 years for the first year, 10 for the second, seven for the third and three for each year following that. A three-year-old dog is 32, a 14-year-old is 65 and our record-setting 34-year-old is an awesome, but more reasonable, 125.

A DREAM LASTS ONLY SECONDS

For years it was believed that no matter how long a dream seemed to last, it actually lasted only a few seconds. This was proven wrong in the 1950s, when scientists learned that the dreaming portion of sleep can be measured by its characteristic REM, or rapid eye movement. We experience REM sleep about five times a night, for longer periods as the night goes on. Our first dream of the night may last only 10 minutes, while the one we finally wake up from may have lasted as long as 45 minutes. The longest dream on record was measured in 1967 at a psychology lab at the University of Illinois, and lasted two hours and 23 minutes. Hopefully it wasn't one of those where you're back in high school, only you've forgotten some critical item of apparel.

DROWNING VICTIMS SURFACE THREE TIMES

According to myth, people who are drowning are supposed to come to the surface three times before finally going under. In the process of drowning, victims tend to breathe water into their lungs each time their heads go underwater. They may then struggle back to the surface any number of times. If they make it back up only twice, no one holds it against them.

EARTHQUAKES OPEN CRACKS
THAT CAN SWALLOW PEOPLE UP

No cinematic earthquake would be complete without a few screaming bodies falling into a widening crack, only to disappear into the bowels of the earth when it closes again. The idea of being swallowed up by the earth must be one of the human race's primordial fears, because it is one of the most commonly expressed concerns about earthquakes despite the fact that it is almost impossible. The cracks earthquakes open up are usually only a few inches wide and not very deep. There was a case in 1948, in Fukui, Japan, when a woman fell up to her chin in a fissure and was crushed to death when the crack closed. She is the only person known to have died this way, although a cow met a similar end in the San Francisco quake of 1906.

Most earthquake deaths are due to the collapse of buildings. In the case of the 1906 quake in San Francisco, nearly all the death and destruction was caused by the fire following the earthquake, not the quake itself.

EATING LIKE A BIRD
MEANS HAVING A SMALL APPETITE

In a creepy moment in *Psycho*, Norman Bates, surrounded by his stuffed aviary, explains that the expression "eats like a bird" is really "a fals-fals-falsity. Because birds really eat a tremendous lot."

Because of their high metabolism, birds eat a great deal more in proportion to their size than do humans, often one-quarter to one-half of their body weight each day. Baby birds eat even more— often as much as their own weight. Granted, that's not much, but still more regurgitated earthworms than you'd care to eat.

EDISON INVENTED THE LIGHTBULB

Edison gets credit for inventing the electric lightbulb in 1879, but almost every element of the design had already been developed by others.

As early as 1802 English chemist Sir Humphrey Davy made an arc lamp glow by passing electricity through a platinum wire. Many consider him the true father of electric light, but he never developed his invention toward any practical end. In 1845 the American J. W. Starr developed an experimental illumination device using a carbon conductor in a vacuum bulb—a very similar design to Edison's. When Starr died at the age of 25, Englishman Joseph Swan continued to work on his concept.

In 1877 Edison began working on the central problem of the lightbulb as a practical source of illumination—the lack of a long-lasting filament. Living up to his credo that "genius is ten percent inspiration, ninety percent perspiration," Edison tried over 8,000 possibilities before arriving at the carbonized cotton thread on October 21, 1879.

Joseph Swan had already arrived at the same solution, demonstrating a carbon filament lamp at Newcastle 10 months earlier. He filed a patent infringement suit against Edison and won. Under the terms of the settlement, Edison took on Swan as a partner in his lighting company, but later bought him out.

Although Edison didn't exactly invent the lightbulb, he deserves full credit for making electrical lighting the enormous success that it is. He organized companies to produce bulbs and developed the equipment necessary for making the system feasible, for example, light sockets. Where would lightbulbs be without them?

EGGS CAN STAND ON END DURING THE EQUINOX

The rumor has it that an egg can be made to balance on end during the vernal equinox. What does it mean? What cosmic forces have lined up to produce this remarkable phenomenon?

The answer is none. If you are patient and steady handed, you can make an egg stand on end anytime. A surface with some grit makes it easier—the trick is usually demonstrated on a sidewalk or in bars, after putting a pinch of salt on the countertop. Give the egg a good, hard shake first—it helps.

EINSTEIN AND CHURCHILL WERE POOR STUDENTS

For years parents of underachievers have found comfort in stories that Einstein and Churchill were slow starters.

Einstein didn't talk until he was three. As legend has it, he did poorly in school and his teachers considered him dull witted. When his parents asked his headmaster what profession he should prepare for, the answer supposedly was: "It doesn't matter; he'll never make a success of anything." He was expelled from high school without a diploma and even failed his college entrance examinations. That part is true, but only because he had trouble learning French. Otherwise, most of the legend derives from a misreading of the grading system at the Swiss school he attended. It has recently been determined that he was doing college level physics by the time he was 11 years old, was gifted at Latin and Greek and was recognized as a "brilliant" violinist.

The myth of Churchill's poor academic performance was largely fostered by his autobiographical *My Early Life*, in which he maintains that he was considered unfit to learn anything but English, and tells the story of how he failed to answer a single question of the Latin portion of his entrance examination for Harrow. That was apparently due to a bad case of test anxiety—Churchill had proven himself a prize student in Latin. According to John Bartlett, headmaster at the elementary school Churchill attended, Churchill was first in his class in every subject except geography, and in that he was second.

ELECTRIC FANS COOL THE AIR

An electric fan cannot cool the air, it can only make you feel cooler by speeding the evaporation of sweat off your body. It may also circulate air from a cooler part of a room to a warmer part. At the same time, the heat of the motor elevates the room temperature, plus there is some small amount of heat generated by the friction of the air against the blades.

ELEPHANTS ARE AFRAID OF MICE; DRINK THROUGH THEIR TRUNKS; NEVER FORGET

The idea that the elephant, largest of all land animals, would be frightened by the mouse, one of the smallest, has a pleasing irony. Unfortunately, it is not true. Elephants have poor eyesight and may

be disturbed by mice rustling in their forage, but they aren't particularly afraid of the little rodents. They've been known to pick mice up with their trunks, examine them and then squash them underfoot.

An elephant uses its trunk to carry water to its mouth, but would be no more comfortable drinking through its trunk than you would be drinking through your nose.

Elephants are intelligent animals that can be trained to remember numerous commands. The idea that they never forget is an exaggeration, though; their memory is no better than that of many other mammals.

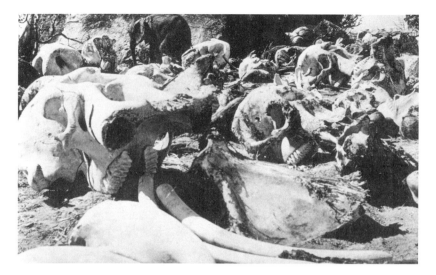

THE ELEPHANTS' GRAVEYARD IS WHERE ELEPHANTS GO TO DIE

When elephants know that the end is near, they are supposed to make their way to a secret graveyard, where they lay down and assume ambient temperature. Like El Dorado, the City of Gold, the thought of an elephants' graveyard fevers men's minds: all that ivory!

The story may have come from finds of multiple elephant remains, possibly due to a herd dying in one place from disease, poisoned water or starvation. Having been featured in the Disney film The Lion King, the myth of the elephants' graveyard is ensured a second life.

Though there is no graveyard, an elephant would be more likely to know when it is about to die than most animals. Elephants that do not die from poachers, predators or disease die of starvation. An elephant uses four huge "cheek teeth" to grind up the 400 to 600 pounds of leaves and bark it eats every day. As these teeth wear out, an elephant is no longer able to chew its food adequately, and a new set of teeth grows in to take their place—up to six times. When the last set wears out, the elephant starves. Lose your bite—lose your life. Seems cruel, but big-game hunter Peter Capstick reminds us that it works the same way on Madison Avenue and Wall Street.

THE EMANCIPATION PROCLAMATION FREED THE SLAVES

Many people think that the Emancipation Proclamation, issued on January 1, 1863, freed the slaves. In fact, it applied only to slaves in the secessionist Southern territories not under U.S. control, and did not free slaves in the four slave states that had remained in the Union. It also had no legal authority and couldn't free Southern slaves any more than a proclamation from the Russian czar could have. Its intention was political rather than moral. In 1862 Lincoln had threatened that those states that did not rejoin the Union would have their slaves freed, and the Emancipation Proclamation was the fulfillment of that threat. Lincoln explained his position in a letter to the *New York Times*: "My paramount objective in this struggle is to save the Union, and is not to save or destroy slavery. If I could save the Union without freeing any slaves I would do it, and if I could save it by freeing all slaves I would do it; and if I could save it by freeing some and leaving others alone I would do that."

The Emancipation Proclamation did have several powerful effects. By guising the Civil War as a crusade against slavery, it helped keep England and France from supporting the Confederacy, as the South hoped they would in order to save their cotton supply. It also opened the way for the recruitment of black soldiers, nearly 180,000 of whom enlisted and fought in the Union Army, an infusion of troops that helped turn the tide of the war.

As the Union Army swept through the South, some 200,000 slaves were freed under the terms of the Emancipation Proclamation as territory was conquered. This was out of a total American slave population of about 4 million, however. It was only after the Thirteenth Amendment was ratified at the end of 1865 that slavery was officially ended.

Lincoln was not the first to use an "Emancipation Proclamation" against his enemies. The British royal governor of Virginia, Lord Dunmore, issued one in 1775, hoping to enlist blacks to fight on Britain's side against Southern patriots, many of whom owned slaves. The proclamation was countermanded by his superiors in London, who considered it needlessly provocative.

ENORMITY IS SYNONYMOUS WITH *ENORMOUSNESS*

Enormity is often used to mean a large quantity of something, as though it were synonymous with *enormousness*. In fact, enormity can only refer to a great deal of evil, as in its most common application, "the enormity of his crimes."

The proper meaning of the word seems lost on most people. One of Bill Clinton's speechwriters used it improperly in a speech, and the President, educated at Georgetown, Yale and Oxford, did not notice the error.

ESKIMOS HAVE A HUNDRED WORDS FOR SNOW WHILE WE HAVE ONLY ONE

This statement is a useful shorthand way of pointing out that people in different situations have different concerns and develop their vocabulary accordingly, but is it true? Laura Martin, professor and head of the Department of Anthropology at Cleveland State University, has a collection of different versions of this saying. In Lanford Wilson's 1978 play *The Fifth of July* the Eskimos are credited with having fifty words for snow. A 1984 *New York Times* editorial mentioned one hundred. Four years its "Science Times" section referred to four dozen. Martin even had a citation of four hundred. Evidently, when you're making a point of this sort, precise figures are of secondary concern.

It may be true that Eskimos have a hundred, or thirty-seven or fourteen words for snow—they can have as many as might occur to them. Eskimos, by which we mean the Inuit and Yupik peoples, speak "polysynthetic" languages, which means you can form new words by adding modifying prefixes and suffixes to any root word. Thus "snow-that-goes-down-your-collar-and-soaks-your-under-

wear" could be constructed as a word in Eskimo parlance. Even so, according to *The Great Eskimo Vocabulary Hoax and Other Irreverent Essays on the Study of Language*, by Geoffrey Pullum, they have far fewer words for the white stuff than we imagine, probably no more than about a dozen if you really stretch it.

At the same time, it's not true that the English language has only one or even a few words for snow. We speak of snow, slush and sleet; of blizzards, flurries and dustings; of hardpack and powder; of snowdrifts and avalanches. There are nearly a hundred terms used by meteorologists and ski-slope operators—it's just that most of us aren't familiar with them. According to Cullen Murphy's "In Praise of Snow" in the January 1995 *Atlantic Monthly*, there are scores of terms just for snow crystals in the atmosphere: "There are needles and sheaths and columns. There are pyramids. Cups. Bullets. Plates. Scrolls. Branches. Dendritic crystals. Stellar crystals." And all of those terms are normally used in combination. "Stellar crystals with plates. Dendritic crystals with branches. Hollow bullets. Bullets with dendrites. Plates with scrolls. Plates with spatial dendrites. Rimed particles. Rimed needle crystals. Lump graupels. Graupel-like snow with nonrimed extensions."

Let's see the Eskimos beat that.

EUNUCHS WERE USED TO GUARD HAREMS BECAUSE THEY WERE IMPOTENT

The eunuch would seem to suffer from one of the more ironic forms of the Catch-22. He was surrounded by beautiful, available women, but in order to get the job he had to surrender his testicles, making it impossible for him to perform sexually, we assume.

Actually, that assumption is incorrect. Though a man without testicles is sterile, in most cases he is perfectly capable of performing sexually. His ability to produce semen, maintain an erection and even ejaculate remains intact. The prostate gland produces a good deal of the ejaculant and the adrenal gland supplies some testosterone.

In ancient Rome testicularly castrated men were called *spadones*. Though they developed a chubby, androgynous appearance, they were in great demand as boy-toys for society ladies whose dalliances had to be discreet.

As far as the harem goes, though, it would be a mistake to imagine that the eunuchs were in any position to have their way.

Knowing full well the capabilities of the testicular eunuch, the harem owner took precautions to prevent employee pilfering. The eunuch's privates were removed in their entirety.

THE EVENING STAR IS A STAR

The star that appears brightly over the western horizon shortly after sunset is often called the evening star. It is not a star at all, but either the planet Venus or Mercury reflecting the sun's illumination.

No wonder nothing happens when you wish upon it.

THE EXCEPTION THAT PROVES THE RULE

The most annoying response someone can give you when you've caught them in an inconsistency is "That's the exception that proves the rule." It's a small step up from "Nyaah-nyaaah!" and hard to argue with because (1) it's an established cliché, and (2) it makes no logical sense. Of course an exception cannot prove a rule—it can only *dis*prove a rule.

The expression in its original meaning was perfectly understandable. *Prove* meant "test." This older meaning survives in expressions such as "proving grounds," where cars are sent to be tested, not to prove that they're good. Another such application is in "the proof of the pudding is in the eating," which means that the pudding is tested when eaten. A test printing of a photograph is likewise called a proof. So the exception *tests* the rule, in that it forces us to examine the rule's validity.

"EYE FOR AN EYE, TOOTH FOR A TOOTH" IS A BIBLICAL PRESCRIPTION FOR HARSH RETRIBUTION

Now that punishment is supposed to be measured and humane, we think of Moses' injunction (Exod. 21:24), "An eye for an eye, a tooth for a tooth," as calling for a rough form of retaliation, as if Ted Bundy should have been be raped, bitten and hacked to death as were his victims. In fact, it was an admonition to keep punishment in proportion to the original offense, and to treat all offenders equally. In Moses' day, a servant or slave could be flogged or killed for a minor offense against a person of higher status.

FEED A COLD, STARVE A FEVER

The biggest problem most of us have with this folk belief is trying to remember which way it goes—is it the cold you feed or the fever? "Feed a fever" has a nicer ring to it, but it's supposed to be the other way.

Fortunately, there's no need to keep this one straight. Sick people should eat when they are hungry, and whether or not they're thirsty, they should drink. Both colds and fevers are best treated with heavy doses of liquid. Don't get your hopes up, though—that liquid shouldn't include a six-pack or two. Alcohol does not replenish the body's fluid, but removes it. It stimulates urination, causing dehydration, and if you tried to subsist solely on alcoholic fluids you'd die of thirst, with or without the cold and fever.

(WE HAVE) FIVE SENSES

Since ancient times, the human body has been described as having five senses, identified as vision, hearing, touch, taste and smell. There is nothing fixed about the number *five*, though. Scientists have come up with a number of other information-gathering faculties of the human body they feel should be identified as senses. These include: balance, pain, temperature, hunger and thirst, "position" senses in muscles that let you know where your hands or feet are without having to look, and a visceral sense that gives us information about our internal organs. There's also that well-known "sixth sense" that tells you which lotto numbers to lose money on.

FORD INVENTED THE AUTOMOBILE, OR AT LEAST THE ASSEMBLY LINE

Those who have not given the matter much thought may assume that Henry Ford invented the automobile. This is not true, of course—the first automobile powered by an internal combustion engine was developed in 1885 by Germany's Gottlieb Daimler and Karl Benz. The first American car was built by Elwood Haynea in 1894.

Ford's great achievement was in making the automobile affordable to the ordinary worker by introducing efficient means of production. He did not, as is commonly believed, invent the assembly line. Ransom E. Olds introduced the assembly line in 1902, raising production at his Olds Motor Vehicle Company from 425 cars to over 2,500 in a single year by assembling cars on rolling platforms. Ford's top engineers designed a moving conveyor belt to assemble his Model T, cutting production time from a day and a half to 93 minutes. The assembly line was a worker's nightmare, and it was in order to hold on to his harried workers that Ford raised the daily pay to an unheard-of $5.

It is commonly believed that the Model T was always available in one color only; supposedly Ford said the customer could have "any color so long as it's black." Actually, the Model T originally came in green with a red stripe. It was only when an astute engineer pointed out that black paint dried more quickly than any other color, allowing for faster production, that the monochromatic policy was adopted.

FOREIGN AID IS A LARGE PART OF THE U.S. BUDGET

When Americans look to places to cut our bloated budget, the most frequently suggested target for trimming is foreign aid. According to polls, many Americans believe that foreign aid accounts for as much as 15 to 20% of the budget. Some retirees when interviewed figured it cost more than their Medicare program. When asked to suggest an appropriate level for foreign aid, "around five percent" was the most common reply. In fact, this would be more than five times the current level of less than 1% of the budget.

Foreign aid looks like a ripe target because it would seem to have no domestic constituency. Actually, that is not true. Due to a 1961 law mandating that payments be spent with U.S. companies if possible, the majority of foreign aid is spent within the borders of the United States, particularly on agricultural products and weapons. The companies that profit from those expenditures lobby for it aggressively. Ironically foreign aid, which would seem the most altruistic of government expenditures, is in many ways a form of corporate welfare.

FORTE IS PRONOUNCED "FORT-AY"

When you're speaking colorfully to impress other people, you may be tempted to toss in the word *forte* to describe someone's strong point. If so, remember that when used in that sense, the word is pronounced "FORT," not "fort-AY." Those in the know will appreciate your erudition, but nine times out of ten your audience will "correct" your pronunciation, somewhat spoiling the effect unless you're into unappreciated one-upmanship.

To confuse the issue, the Italian musical term *forte*, meaning "loudly" or "with force," *is* pronounced "for-TAY."

FORTY YEARS OLD WAS
CONSIDERED ELDERLY IN THE PAST

Those who have entered their 40s are sometimes reminded that they should count themselves lucky—after all, a 40-year-old was considered elderly in the past.

This is a misinterpretation of statistical data. It is true that 200 years ago, the average life span in North America was about 35 to 40 years. Two thousand years ago it was 20 to 25 years. But that cannot be taken to mean that people who exceeded the average life span were considered old. The average life span is determined by the ages of all those who die, and that figure is dramatically affected by the rate of infant mortality. Most deaths are clustered at two age levels: under one year of age and over age 75. Reduce the number at the lower end and you'll increase the number at the higher.

Obviously, our ancestors were unprotected against diseases for which we have vaccinations and treatments, but the tough ones who fended off those threats were entirely capable of living as long as we do. Even disregarding unprovable claims of extreme longevity (Methuselah, for example), there are plenty of documented cases of people in the past living over 100 years. There was a French man, Pierre Joubert, who was born on July 15, 1701, and died November 16, 1814, aged 113 years and 124 days. Of our first half-dozen presidents,

George Washington lived to age 67, John Adams lived to 91, Jefferson to 83, Madison to 85, Monroe to 73 and John Quincy Adams to 81.

You may think that these men of privilege cannot be considered typical. Unlike the average guy, they had access to the finest medical care available. Read a little about eighteenth- and nineteenth-century medicine and you will agree that the less access you had to it, the better.

FRANKENSTEIN WAS A MONSTER

The monster we think of as Frankenstein is really Frankenstein's monster—Victor Frankenstein was the mad scientist. It wasn't "Dr." Frankenstein either—in Mary Shelley's story he hadn't even been to medical school.

As for the monster, in the original story he's no dope. He speaks French, reads Milton and studies Plutarch—the sort of strong classical education that today's average college student spends four years avoiding.

BEN FRANKLIN DISCOVERED ELECTRICITY WHEN HIS KITE WAS STRUCK BY LIGHTNING

Benjamin Franklin did not discover electricity, though he did experiment with it and came up with many of the terms still in use today. The Greeks were aware of static electricity, which they generated by rubbing amber with fur (the word *electric* comes from *elektron*, Greek for "amber").

In his famous 1752 experiment, Franklin was seeking to prove the electrical nature of lightning, and did so when a static spark flew to his knuckle from a key tied to the kite string. Contrary to the popular image, Franklin's kite was not struck by lightning—if it had been, it might have been the end of the prolific inventor, author, printer, publisher, Founding Father and notorious party animal. The spark was generated by the flow of electrons that exists at all times between the sky and the ground, which is displayed most dramatically during a thunderstorm.

Franklin went on to invent the lightning rod. He was fortunate he did not become one.

THE FULL MOON MAKES PEOPLE ACT CRAZY

It's a well-known fact among cops and emergency-room workers that the full moon brings out the crazies. In fact, the word *lunatic* comes from the Latin word for the moon, so the idea's been around for quite a while. It's a hard one to argue with. When strange behavior coincides with the full moon, people are sure to remark on it, and when it doesn't, of course, they don't.

Statistics that claim to support the full moon hypothesis fall apart on examination. One such study chose periods in which full moons fell disproportionately on weekends, when an upsurge in strange happenings can always be expected. In 1985 two scientists decided to put the matter to rest. Studying the correlation between the full moon and crime, suicide, psychiatric admissions, etc., they found it amounted to no more than 0.03% of the monthly variation. That is surprisingly small—one would expect that the extra illumination the full moon provides during the wee hours would be enough to spike a more significant increase in mischief.

FULTON INVENTED THE STEAMBOAT; IT WAS CALLED THE *CLERMONT*

Most of the fame and fortune attached to any great innovation goes not to the remarkable mind that made the fundamental breakthrough, but to the marketing genius who figured out how to make it pay.

There is no way to successfully argue that Robert Fulton invented the steamboat in 1807. James Rumsey demonstrated a crude steamboat on the Potomac in 1784. John Fitch demonstrated a 45-foot steamboat, with a top speed of 8 mph, to the Continental Congress in 1787. Five years later he put an improved model on the Delaware River to provide regular passenger service between Philadelphia, Pennsylvania, and Trenton, New Jersey. His claim to the invention was challenged by Rumsey, but Fitch was granted the U.S. patent in 1791. Unfortunately his venture was not a success, nor were several others that followed his.

Fulton did what no one else had been able to—he established the first *successful* steamboat line, providing regular service on the Hudson River between New York and Albany. His boat was called *North River Steamboat*, not the *Clermont*. The town of Clermont, New York, was the first port on its route and gave the boat its nickname.

Fulton was clearly entitled to the fortune his enterprise brought him, but why the glory? John Fitch, the true visionary, died broke nine years before Fulton launched his steamboat, suffering from the tragic flaw that dooms so many to obscurity—lack of marketing expertise.

THE FUNNY BONE IS SENSITIVE TO PAIN

Can the funny bone feel pain? The bone that runs from your shoulder to your elbow is called the *humerus*, and if it feels any pain it's over the lame pun on its name. The painful twinge you get when you bump your elbow has nothing to do with the bone. It comes from the ulnar nerve, the main nerve running through your arm. It is near the surface and unprotected at the elbow.

GAY HAS ONLY RECENTLY BEEN USED TO DESCRIBE SEXUAL ORIENTATION

The use of the word *gay* for homosexual would strike most people as a recent development, and many have expressed frustration that they can no longer use the word in its older sense without creating confusion, as in "don we now our gay apparel," etc. *Gay* has actually been around in its present usage since the early 1900s, and some linguists date it back to Elizabethan England. In Shakespeare's day male actors played both the male and female roles, show business being considered too wicked for the womenfolk. The young men who played the parts of women and girls were known as the *gaieties*, which was shortened to *gays*.

Not quite as old is *dyke*, for lesbian. This has been around since the early 1800s as a contraction of dike-jumper. A dike-jumper was one who crossed a boundary into a different field, in this case a sexual boundary.

A fair amount of confusion also surrounds the word *homosexual*. It might seem to mean "lover of men." However, the *homo-* in homosexual is not the same as the *homo* in *homo sapiens*—it does not mean "man." "Homosexual" was clumsily cobbled together from the Greek word *homos*, meaning "same" (as in "homogeneous"), and the

Latin word *sexualis*. In its proper meaning, *homosexual* applies to all same-sex relationships, either male-male or female-female. It is our confusion over the meaning of the word *homo* in this context that has led to the retention of a separate term for female homosexuals.

GERMS CAUSE BAD BREATH

A popular mouthwash claims that it "kills the germs that cause bad breath," but most bad breath does not come from the mouth. The breath odor associated with onions or garlic comes from volatile oils in those foods, which enter the bloodstream and are transported to the lungs. There they mix with carbon dioxide and are exhaled. The smell comes from the lungs, not from the mouth itself. The same is true of bad breath associated with cigarette smoking.

The mouth is actually an ideal environment for microbes and provides a home to billions of them. Over 10 million bacteria may live in a single drop of saliva. Most of the bacteria in the mouth is unaffected by a mouthwash because it is safely hidden in inaccessible areas, such as beneath the gum line. Mouthwash may kill off a certain amount of bacteria, but the levels begin returning to normal soon after the mouthwash is spit out. A good thing too—bacteria serves a useful purpose in the digestive process.

True halitosis is caused by tooth decay, gum problems or infections, and can only be treated by a dentist. All mouthwash can do is cosmetically cover up an odor, much like an air freshener masks unpleasant odors with its own perfume.

THE GREAT WALL OF CHINA IS THE ONLY MAN-MADE OBJECT VISIBLE FROM SPACE

During an uneventful space shuttle mission (is that redundant?), as the *Columbia* passed over mainland China, ABC's Peter Jennings made the well-worn observation that "the Great Wall of China is the only man-made object visible from outer space."

Like so many things we hear on the nightly news, a moment's consideration would reveal this to be preposterous. Why would the Great Wall be any more visible than that gigantic shopping mall outside of Minneapolis? Because it's *longer*? Is a thread more visible at 10 feet than, say, a raisin?

The notoriously unreliable *Ripley's Believe It or Not!* was the apparent source of this chestnut, originally claiming that the Great

Wall would be mankind's only creation visible from the moon. When asked about this, the astronaut Captain Alan Bean replied that from the moon, all you can see of Earth is a sphere covered mostly by white clouds, with blue oceans and some yellow deserts and green vegetation visible. Even at a height of a few thousand miles, no man-made object is visible, he reported.

At an altitude of a hundred miles or so, all sorts of large man-made objects are visible—cities, dams, highway cloverleaves, large ships at sea, Pamela Anderson's bust, etc.

GREEK STATUARY WAS WHITE STONE

When a wealthy Saudi Arabian bought a mansion on Sunset Boulevard for his 23-year-old son, he had no idea how innovative his son's decorating plans would be. Crowds gathered on the side-walk and gaped after its white neoclassical statues were painted in flesh tones, with nipples and pubic hair included. Complaints poured into City Hall that someone would reduce Greek statuary to such a vulgar level. The $2.4 million estate became such an icon of bad taste that it was featured in Steve Martin's *The Jerk*.

Those who thought that the painting was the work of a jerk might have been surprised to learn that the statuary was actually made more authentic. The ancient Greeks did not leave their sculp-ture white, but painted it colorfully. The Parthenon itself was bright-ly colored in its heyday.

GROUND ZERO MEANS A STARTING POINT

We've all heard politicians say that we have to start over "from ground zero." The cliché they're usually searching for is "from square one." Ground zero refers to the target of a bomb, usually a nuclear bomb. Activity is more likely to end at ground zero than to begin there.

THE GUILLOTINE WAS AN INVENTION OF THE FRENCH REVOLUTION

The guillotine seemed to come along just in time for the French Revolution, what with all the deadwood nobility that needed pruning. It was named for Joseph Ignace Guillotine, a physician and member of the French National Assembly. The story is that he invented it as a more humane form of execution than what had gone on before—the hacking off of heads by inexperienced executioners who might require a half-dozen strokes to get the job done.

Though the guillotine was named for Dr. Guillotine, it was not his invention. He proposed it, but a Dr. Antonin Louis actually designed and built the device, which was initially called a *louisette* or *louison*. Somehow Guillotine's name came to be attached to the head-chopper—perhaps *louisette* sounded inappropriately wimpy. The family was not especially pleased with the honor; after the doctor's death in 1814 (not, as rumor has it, on his namesake) his children changed the

family name to escape the association.

Devices like the guillotine had been around for centuries, including examples in England, Ireland and Scotland, where a decapitator called "The Maiden" is still on display at the National Museum of Antiquities in Edinburgh. Why was it called "The Maiden"? So that if you asked, they could point out that men have been known to lose their heads over maidens too.

HAIR AND FINGERNAILS
CONTINUE TO GROW AFTER DEATH

The idea that hair and fingernails continue to grow after death is one of those macabre facts we pick up on the playground and treasure in the knowledge that we can soon spring it on someone else. It's been around for a long time, and several accounts seem to support it. Elizabeth Siddal, model and wife of the Pre-Raphaelite painter-poet Dante Gabriel Rossetti, was exhumed seven years after her burial in order to retrieve the only complete manuscript of Rossetti's poems, which the grief-stricken widower had placed in her coffin. It is said that her strawberry-blond hair nearly filled the coffin. If so, it must have done so at the time she was interred, since neither hair nor fingernails grow on a dead body.

After death, the soft tissues of a corpse shrink as they dry out, exposing an extra fraction of an inch on the length of hair, fingernails and toenails. This might give the illusion of growth in the case of a man with a clean-shaven face.

Whatever your plans for the afterlife, they need not include barbers, hairdressers or manicurists.

HAIR CAN TURN WHITE OVERNIGHT FROM SHOCK

This is another staple of low-rent horror yarns: "When they forced open the oaken doors of the mausoleum, Lord Chauncy staggered out, ashen-faced and trembling. His rescuers gasped in astonishment at his hair—it had turned snowy white in a single night..."

In *The Prisoner of Chillon* (1816), Byron employs the image:
My hair is gray, but not with years,
Nor grew it white
In a single night,
As men's have grown from sudden fears.

These dated sources shouldn't surprise anyone, but the same shtick was dusted off in the 1995 weepie, *Legends of the Fall*.

Hair cannot turn gray or white overnight. The color of your hair is determined by differing amounts of the pigment called melanin. As you get older, your melanin-producing cells shrink and produce less pigment, so that the hair is no longer colored as it grows. The white or gray appearance of the hair is simply its natural color without pigment added.

There is still anecdotal evidence to the contrary. When President Reagan had his head shaved for surgery, his normally orangey black hair grew back gray, to the astonishment of everyone. Since we had always been told that he didn't color it, the Reagan phenomenon defies explanation.

HALF OF ALL MARRIAGES END IN DIVORCE

This is the sort of statement that gives statistics a bad name. This figure is reached by comparing the number of marriages every year to the number of divorces; there are nearly half as many divorces as marriages. But what does that mean? Not, as it implies, that half of all people who get married will end up getting divorced. Some people marry and divorce several times, seriously skewing the stats. A few like Elizabeth Taylor, Mickey Rooney, Zsa Zsa Gabor and Larry King can really throw things out of whack. If you averaged them in with four people who'd remained married for a lifetime, you'd conclude that 85% of all marriages end in divorce.

Of new marriages, about one in four will end in divorce.

A HANDSHAKE IS LESS LIKELY
TO SPREAD GERMS THAN A KISS

During cold season, many people are reluctant to greet friends with a kiss, preferring the less risky handshake. In fact, when it comes to transmission of the cold virus, a handshake is far more likely to pass it along than a kiss. You're far more likely to pick up a cold through hand contact than by being directly coughed or sneezed upon. Medical researchers at the University of Virginia found that the cold virus exists in such low concentrations in saliva that sneezes or coughs would transmit it only 10% of the time. The virus was found on the hands of 65% of cold sufferers, though, and handshakes passed along the virus in 70% of cases. After shaking

hands, the uninfected parties then touched their eyes or noses, the location of the mucous membranes, which picked up the disease.

Pucker up, but keep your hands to yourself.

HICCUPS CAN BE CURED BY A SUDDEN SHOCK

The cause of hiccups is mysterious, and unlike coughing, gagging and vomiting, the reflex serves no discernible purpose. The classic home remedy is a sudden shock, which many people believe may break the pattern by distracting the hiccups sufferer. In prolonged bouts of hiccuping this cure has proven as ineffective as any other. Other common remedies include breathing in and out of a paper bag, holding your breath for a minute, swallowing a teaspoon of sugar, and drinking water from the far side of a cup. Some of the weirder modern strategies include massaging the carotid artery in the neck, carefully tickling the eardrum with a hair, and tapping rhythmically on the fifth vertebra in the neck.

The longest bout of hiccups on record was suffered by Charles Osborne of Anthon, Iowa, who hiccuped every 1 1/2 seconds for 69 years and 5 months, from 1922 until 1990. During that time he tried every known cure, without effect.

The fact that there are so many remedies for hiccups indicates that none of them really work; otherwise, there would only be one.

THE HIMALAYAN MOUNTAIN RANGE IS THE GREATEST ON EARTH

The Himalayan mountain range is a mere 1,600 miles long, while the longest mountain range on Earth extends more than 10,000 miles and is from 300 to 600 miles wide. It's called the Mid-Atlantic Ridge and stretches under the Atlantic Ocean from Iceland nearly down to the Antarctic Circle.

Most of the mountains lie entirely underwater, but the tops of some of the tallest peaks break the surface. They are the islands known as the Azores, Ascension, St. Paul and St. Helena. Pico Island in the Azores rises 27,000 feet from the ocean floor (the same height as Mt. Everest), and 7,615 feet of that is above sea level.

HITLER WAS A HOUSE PAINTER OR WALLPAPER HANGER; HIS REAL NAME WAS SHICKLGRUBER; HE DANCED A JIG AFTER THE FALL OF FRANCE

Wartime propaganda tried to make Hitler the subject of ridicule, rather than terror, through a number of fairly childish untruths.

—It was claimed that Hitler's former occupation had been as a house painter or wallpaper hanger. In *Patton*, some troops ask the general where he's headed, and he answers that he's on his way to Berlin to "personally shoot that paper-hanging sonuvabitch." As a matter of fact, Hitler never pursued either profession. He was a frustrated but not untalented watercolor artist.

—A lot of derisive mileage was gotten out of the suggestion that *Der Führer*'s real name was "Shicklgruber." Although that silly-sounding name figured in Hitler's ancestry, the family name was Hitler when Adolf was born, and he was never known by any other.

—After the French surrender in 1940, newsreels in America showed Hitler dancing a ridiculous "victory jig." This bit of footage, which still shows up in World War II retrospectives, was faked. A loop was made of a single small hop and repeated to create the

Charlie Chaplin ridiculed Hitler in *The Great Dictator.*

effect, much as in those commercials where a cat does the cha-cha-cha. The purpose, according to Laurence Stallings, editor in chief of the Movietone newsreel system, was to make Hitler look like "the sissiest, most ludicrous conqueror that ever lived."

There are those who don't realize that Hitler wasn't German by birth, but Austrian.

HOLLAND IS THE HOME OF TULIPS AND THE LITTLE DUTCH BOY WHO PUT HIS FINGER IN THE DIKE

—Tulips have been associated with Holland for 400 years, but they were not native to it. They originated in Asia and North Africa, and the first bulbs were brought to Europe from Turkey in the 1550s.
—The tale of the little Dutch boy who saved his town by plugging a leak in a dike with his finger has been familiar to Americans for some time; considerably longer than it's been familiar to the Dutch, in fact. The story first appeared in *Hans Brinker; or The Silver Skates*, an 1865 book by Mary Mapes Dodge, an American. The Dutch had never heard the story until American tourists began asking what dike it was that the plucky little lad stuck his finger in. Annoyed with this nonsense at first, the Dutch eventually caved in. They erected a statue of him near the Spaarndem lock, presumably to honor him for attracting so many gullible, free-spending visitors.

HOLLYWOOD SIGN WAS PUT
UP TO HONOR THE MOVIE INDUSTRY

When it was built, the famous HOLLYWOOD sign had nothing to do with the movie industry. The sign originally spelled out "HOLLYWOODLAND" and was erected near the top of Mt. Cahuenga in 1924 to promote a large real-estate subdivision overlooking Sunset Boulevard, Hollywood's main drag. Each white sheet-metal letter was nearly 50 feet tall and about 30 feet wide. Outlined with light bulbs, the sign could be seen for miles, day or night, and soon became associated with the movie industry. In September 1932, Lillian Millicent "Peg" Entwhistle, an actress down on her luck, jumped to her death from the letter *H*.

Fifteen years after it was built, maintenance on the sign was discontinued and it fell into disrepair. All 8,000 of its 20-watt lightbulbs were stolen. In 1945 the development company donated it along with several hundred adjoining acres to the city's Parks and Recreation Department. Four years later the *H* blew down. Though many felt that the sign was an eyesore and should be removed entirely, the Parks Commission finally decided to repair the first nine letters and remove the last four. Since then the sign has had more ups and downs than John Travolta's career. Fortunately, the show-biz community has always come through with sufficient donations to sustain it. After all, since 1973 the sign has been recognized as an official Historic Cultural Monument, and L.A. has few of those to spare.

HORNS AND ANTLERS ARE SYNONYMOUS;
ONLY MALES HAVE ANTLERS; THE
RHINOCEROS HAS A TRUE HORN

Although horns and antlers serve the same purpose in the animal world, the two are not the same. Horns have a bony core and grow throughout an animal's life. Antlers are made of a hardened skin material and are shed and regrown annually, even the most impressive racks. Antlers may branch out as they grow, but horns never do.

When you see a deer with antlers, it's safe to assume that it's a male, right? Only as long as it's not a reindeer or caribou. Reindeer and caribou of both sexes bear antlers, though at different times of the year.

The rhinoceros' horn is not a horn at all, but matted hair that is hardened by secretions of keratin, the same stuff that fingernails are made of. As a means of self-protection it couldn't be more counterproductive—the Asian belief that powdered rhinoceros horn is an aphrodisiac has resulted in the near-extinction of the species.

THE HUMAN BODY RENEWS ITSELF EVERY SEVEN YEARS

It is said that cells in the human body are replaced in seven-year cycles, so that the body you're in now is completely different than the one you occupied seven years ago. This belief has even been suggested as a rationale for statutes of limitations—it would be unfair to prosecute someone for a crime that was, in a sense, committed by a "different" person.

The idea is hogwash, of course. The human body changes constantly, but it's not renewed every seven years. Some parts of the body don't change at all, or else you'd periodically lose those coffee stains on your teeth, as well as that decorative scarification you had done in Mali 10 years ago. *Seven* is just one of those numbers to which all sorts of mystical qualities are attributed. You have your seven virtues, seven years of bad luck, seven seals, seven ages of man, seven dwarfs, etc.

THE HUMAN BODY WOULD EXPLODE IN A VACUUM

In *Total Recall*, Hollywood showed us in great gory detail what would happen to the human body if it were caught in the vacuum of an airless planet—the belly distends grotesquely, cheeks puff out and eyes swell up and explode like stepped-on grapes. It put to shame the wimpy *2001*, where astronaut Bowman actually survives a few seconds in the vacuum of space. Viewers may have assumed that the movies just couldn't do it right until the special-effects wizards got their act together.

According to scientists, though, the *2001* version is the more accurate. The human body is remarkably tough and would resist deformation even in a complete vacuum. You would have about seven to 15 seconds of "useful consciousness" in which you might be able to get yourself to safety, as did the helmetless astronaut. The air would be sucked from your lungs and your eardrums might rupture. Death would follow in minutes, but at least you'd retain possession of your eyeballs, according to a space-medicine expert at Cape Canaveral. The human body suffers another unfortunate side effect from being in a vacuum, says the same expert, but in that regard you can take comfort in this cosmic truth: "In space, no one can hear you fart."

HUMANS USE ONLY 10% OF THEIR BRAINS

This statement has been around for a hundred years or so, with different specified percentages. The pioneering psychologist and philosopher William James wrote in *The Energies of Men* (1908): "We are making use of only a small part of our possible mental and physical resources." Anthropologist Margaret Mead is supposed to have said we only use 6%. The implication is that you could really be hot stuff if only you could figure out how to tap into that remaining 90% or so. Telekinesis, teleportation, psi forces—all those mutant comic-book-hero capabilities could be at your command. Or at least you could locate that great novel you know is in your head somewhere, and have enough smarts left over to negotiate a good movie deal.

The fact is, scientists doubt that we have much unutilized gray matter. While no more than 5% of the brain may be used at any one time, that's because the parts of the brain are specialized, with different parts used for different activities. Scientists who have figured out the function of each part of the brain have not turned up any large unused areas. During any given activity you may be using only a small part of your brain, but you probably use most of it during the course of a day, unless you're watching soap operas.

HUMIDITY—WHEN IT'S 100%, IT'S RAINING

When the humidity is 100%, it's not raining, it's foggy.

HYENAS SCAVENGE THE LIONS' PREY

It was long believed that hyenas lived solely off whatever they could beg, borrow or steal of what lions had killed. This fit in with the popular image of the lion as the noble beast and the hyena as the despised scavenger, reprised most recently in Disney's *The Lion King*.

The July 1968 *National Geographic* reports that the reality is otherwise. Hyenas are skilled hunters in their own right, able to run down and kill large wildebeest and zebras. Generally, lions and hyenas each do their own killing, but each will attempt to steal carcasses from the other. Often it is the lions who steal the hyenas' kill, and if the hyenas cannot fight them off they have to wait until the lions leave in order to eat the supper they earned. The *Geographic* described one such tactical retreat, after which a busload of tourists happened on the scene and one said contemptuously of the hyenas, "Look at them—they're waiting for the spoils."

It's tough to shuck a bad reputation.

IF ONLY ONE LIFE IS SAVED, IT'S WORTH IT

This statement is often used to defend a law or regulation against critics who claim that it is too costly. As an emotional appeal it is hard to argue with, but in almost every case, legislation defended on this basis deserves a more critical look. For example, the National Transportation Safety Board and the Association of Flight Attendants pushed for legislation that would have required that infants and small children sit in a child safety seat while traveling by plane, rather than on their parents' lap. They argued that a child in a protective seat is much safer in the event of an airplane crash. Of course, the airlines could also then sell an extra ticket. When critics pointed to the increased costs—an average of $200 per family per trip—the defenders were quick to resort to the handy "If only one child's life is saved, it will be worth it." Who wants to make a cost-benefit argument when the benefit is the life of a child? But there is an argument to be made, and it ultimately caused the FAA to decline to press for such legislation. Due to the cost of buying tickets for one or two small children, it is estimated that 20% of families would choose to drive rather than fly across country while on vacation. With highway fatality rates much higher than those for airlines, it was calculated that this would result in an increase of 82 infant deaths over a 10-year period. Transportation Secretary Frederico Pena concluded that requiring safety seats to be used on airplanes would thereby cause more deaths and injuries than it would prevent.

The same reasoning can be applied to most cases where this argument is used. Resources are limited, and when considering the cost of any legislation that might "save one life," it's important to ask whether the same resources could save more lives if applied elsewhere. Everything in life is a trade-off. The 55 mph speed limit has been defended on the basis that it has saved lives. But how many more lives could be saved if we dropped the limit to 35 mph? For many of us, if we had to drive that slowly on our superhighways, life just wouldn't be worth living anyway.

INFERTILE COUPLES WHO ADOPT A CHILD ARE THEN MORE LIKELY TO CONCEIVE

Everyone knows of a couple that, unable to conceive a child, adopted one only to have the wife become pregnant a short time thereafter. The observation has become a truism, explained with a kind of pseudo-logic: having adopted, the couple is now "relaxed" about having a child, and for that reason is somehow more likely to conceive one of their own.

Research on this phenomenon has turned up no evidence to support it. Childless couples who adopt are no more likely to conceive thereafter than those who do not. It is simply that the circumstance grabs our attention and therefore impresses itself upon us. In that way it is like other such observations: "I always pick the slowest checkout line at the supermarket," or "Whenever I learn a new word I always hear it used within a few days." We don't even notice those cases where an adoptive couple does not conceive, we move right along in the supermarket line or we never hear a newly learned word again. Those occasions are unmemorable and therefore not remembered.

IT'S NOT WORTH IT TO PICK UP A PENNY ANYMORE

In the last few years it has become common to see pennies lying on the sidewalk. It's generally regarded as not worth the trouble to pick them up, even by the average panhandler. Is it? Figuring that it shouldn't take you more than three seconds to pick up a penny, that works out to 20¢ a minute, or $12 an hour. Whether that's worth your time depends on what you earn. If you won't bother to pick up a dime, you must really be raking it in.

IVAN THE TERRIBLE MUST HAVE BEEN A TERRIBLE FELLOW

Back before politicians had to periodically run for office, they were able to show their true natures, and it wasn't a pretty sight. Nevertheless, we would figure a guy had to be unusually fiendish to acquire a moniker like "Ivan the Terrible." That assumption is based on a mistranslation of the Russian word *grozny*, which is meant to suggest awe rather than terror. "Ivan the Awesome" would be more like it. Granted, Ivan the Terrible was no Phil Donahue—he ordered his share of torture and executions and had the tongue of a nobleman cut out after he spoke rudely to him (if Donahue did that he'd clobber Oprah in the ratings). As absolute monarchs went, though, the first tsar of Russia was no more frightening than his contemporaries.

JAPAN HAS NO ARMY; MIXED NUDE BATHING; HIGH SUICIDE RATE, ETC.

Though Japan is less exotic to the average American now than it was 30 years ago, numerous misconceptions remain. For example, contrary to popular belief, there *are* stupid, lazy Japanese people; in fact, hundreds of them. There are other falsehoods:.

—Japan's constitution, imposed upon the country during the American occupation, stipulated that Japan would maintain only "self-defense forces" and would spend no more than 1.5% of its gross national product on its military. This limitation, and the fact that the United States continues to station thousands of troops there, has caused many to assume that Japan's military might is negligible. Its nervous Asian neighbors know otherwise. Because Japan's GNP is so enormous, even a tiny percentage of it gives Japan the third largest military budget in the world. Japan's armed forces number about 250,000 highly trained volunteers armed with the latest weaponry. Figures on the navy from 1989 list 14 submarines and 60 destroyers and frigates. The air force has over 300 modern jet aircraft.

—The Japanese are still not plentifully supplied with hot water in their homes, and many families visit public baths daily. To the disappointment of many male tourists, however, the sexes are separated. Mixed nude bathing is decidedly a thing of the past. You'd be more likely to encounter it in California, or even Idaho.

—One thing we all know about Japan is its high suicide rate, and it seems only fair that a nation that seems to work so well should have a dark underside. The Japanese may not kill each other at the rate we do, but they kill *themselves*. Furthermore, suicide is part of their tradition—hara-kiri, the samurai ethic and all that. The fact is, however, that the Japanese suicide rate, about 17 per 100,000, is lower than that of numerous other countries. Denmark's rate is 26 per 100,000. Among industrialized nations,

Austria, Switzerland, West Germany, Hungary and Czechoslovakia all have higher suicide rates than Japan's.

While on the topic, most Americans don't realize that even though we kill each other with abandon, we still pile up more suicides than homicides every year.

—In the post-war period, when "Made in Japan" was associated with manufactured goods of the poorest quality, a rumor abounded that the Japanese had named one of their cities "USA" just so they could stamp their shoddy merchandise with the prestigious label "Made in USA." The rumor overlooked the fact that products are not stamped with the city of origin, and it is unlikely that U.S. Customs would smile benignly on such a ruse. Where did it come from? Probably from the fact that there actually is a small city in Japan called Usa. Any subterfuge in its name would be subtle indeed, as it predates the founding of the U.S.A. by several centuries.

Ironically, a similar ruse was actually used *against* the Japanese. The Matsui brand, with its rising sun symbol, is owned by Curry's, a British electronics company. It uses no Japanese components. The made-up name was intended to be "a bit mystical and foreign-sounding," according to the company, professing innocence as to any duplicitous intent. The company was forced to drop its original, misleading slogan, "Japanese Technology Made Perfect."

JEFFERSON HAD A LONG AFFAIR WITH HIS SLAVE SALLY HEMMINGS

The 1995 film *Jefferson in Paris* is based on the rumor that Thomas Jefferson had a long-standing relationship with one of his slaves, Sally Hemmings, and fathered five children by her. This story cannot be repudiated, but it has never been proven and there is plenty of reason to doubt it.

The story was first published in 1802 by James T. Callender, a bitter political rival, along with every other scandalous rumor about Jefferson he could get his hands on. Then in 1873, an Ohio newspaper published an interview with a slave named Madison Hemmings who claimed that Jefferson was his father, though of course there was no way he could prove it. A rival editor noted wryly that, though Madison would have been present at his own birth, "his extreme youth would prevent him from knowing all the facts connected with that important event." According to the editor, slave mothers often claimed illustrious fathers for their children. Fawn Brodie's *Thomas Jefferson: An Intimate Biography*, published in 1974, claimed not only that the relationship was real, but that it lasted 38 years. Brodie's assertion relies on her interpretations of circumstantial evidence: Sally Hemmings was an acknowledged beauty, Jefferson was home at the time each of her children would have been conceived, they were given special treatment and they were the only slaves Jefferson freed. One is said to have closely resembled him.

There is also evidence against the allegation. Historian Dumas Malone, one of the foremost Jefferson authorities, says that the man would never have done anything as tawdry as have sex with a woman who was not in a position to say no. (Apparently politicians were different in those days.) Jefferson would also have had to have fathered two of the children after the scandal broke, while he was President, a level of brashness we would hardly expect of Bill Clinton. Jefferson's family would have presumably been upset by such an obvious, ongoing dalliance, but there is no evidence of any domestic discord. Those who worked at Monticello, as well as two of his grandchildren, all believed that Hemmings' children were fathered by Jefferson's nephews, Peter and Samuel Carr. That would explain any family resemblance.

JESUS WAS BORN BY IMMACULATE CONCEPTION, CATHOLICS BELIEVE

The Catholic Church's doctrine of the immaculate conception does not apply to Jesus' conception, but to his mother Mary's. Furthermore, it doesn't necessarily mean that her parents didn't conceive her in the usual fashion—it says that Mary was born without Original Sin "thanks to a grace given in the first moment of her existence" by God.

The doctrine of the immaculate conception began as a folk belief in the eighth century and was made an article of faith by Pope Pius IX in 1854. He also declared the doctrine of papal infallibility, but since the doctrine of the immaculate conception predated that by 16 years you'll have to use your judgment.

What is usually meant by the immaculate conception is actually a separate doctrine, the Virgin Birth of Christ.

THE JUGULAR VEIN IS THE MAIN CONDUIT OF BLOOD THROUGH THE NECK; CUTTING IT CAUSES A QUICK DEATH

The expression "to go for the jugular" suggests that there is one

vein called the jugular, but there are actually from three to five different veins in the neck area that can be called jugular veins, depending on which anatomy book you rely on. The largest two are the left and right interior jugulars, which run along either side of the neck. They're the ones that Dracula goes for.

The other error implicit in the expression is that the jugular is a vital lifeline, and that severing it would cause instant death. The jugulars drain deoxygenated blood from the brain, and a cut in them could only cause death if air was sucked into the vein. The flow from a cut jugular can be stanched by pressing a finger against it.

What *would* cause a quick death is cutting one of the two carotid arteries, which feed blood to the brain at high pressure. They produce the great jets of blood familiar to viewers of samurai films.

JULIUS CAESAR WAS A ROMAN EMPEROR; GAVE HIS NAME TO THE CESAREAN SECTION

—Julius Caesar was never called that by his countrymen. He was just plain Caesar. Back then a man was not called by his first name unless it was necessary to distinguish him from his siblings.

—Caesar was also never an emperor. Rome was still a republic in his day, though he helped to bring about the republic's fall.

—The belief that the caesarean section was named after Caesar, because he was born in that fashion, is incorrect. No one knows in what manner Caesar was delivered, but it was probably not surgically. The operation was performed at the time, but usually only to rescue the infant when a mother died in childbirth. It was not normally performed on a healthy mother, and Caesar's mother lived a good many years after his birth. Ignorance of sterile surgical techniques at the time makes that seem unlikely. The operation was not named after Caesar—it got its name from the Latin word *caedere*, "to cut."

—Neither was the Caesar salad named after the Roman general. It was named for its creator, Caesar Gardini, who came up with the cold plate at his Caesar's Place Restaurant in Tijuana, Mexico.

JUMPING UP IN A FALLING ELEVATOR MIGHT ENABLE YOU TO ESCAPE DEATH

This may not exactly be a belief—more like wishful thinking. The question is, if you were on an elevator free-falling down its shaft, should you keep on eye on those floor-indicator lights and leap into the air just as you're about to hit bottom? Sorry, it won't work. After three seconds of free fall, the elevator would reach a downward velocity of 96 feet per second. Your upward leap might achieve a velocity of 14 feet per second, leaving you still heading downward at a net velocity of 82 feet per second. The guy who'll scrape you off the floor will never notice the difference.

If, precisely at the moment of impact, you were able to instantly accelerate upward at 96 feet per second, even that would not help. Such a sudden acceleration would crush your body as effectively as would impact with the floor.

KENNEDY COINED THE STATEMENT: "ASK NOT WHAT YOUR COUNTRY CAN DO FOR YOU; ASK WHAT YOU CAN DO FOR YOUR COUNTRY"

The most stirring words from John F. Kennedy's inaugural address are often credited to him, but they have a long history. In an 1884 address, the great Supreme Court justice Oliver Wendell Holmes, Jr. implored his audience "...to recall what our country has done

for each of us, and to ask ourselves what we can do for our country in return." The words sound even more like those of a speech delivered at a political convention in 1916: "We must have a citizenship less concerned about what the government can do for it and more anxious about what it can do for the nation." That speech was given by a man who is now considered to be one of the worst presidents in the nation's history, and a Republican to boot. The Kennedys would like to keep that association under wraps. Lifting a line from Oliver Wendell Holmes is one thing, but—Warren G. Harding?!

Civil libertarians have never been too crazy about the hallowed sentiment either. If you think about it, it could easily have been uttered by any of the world's most repressive dictators.

KENNEDY WAS THE HERO OF PT-109; AUTHOR OF *PROFILES IN COURAGE*; YOUNGEST PRESIDENT; A LIBERAL PRESIDENT

Outside of Washington and Lincoln, no President is so shrouded in myth as is John F. Kennedy. It was a combination of several factors: his glamour and charisma; the popularity he enjoyed with the press and intelligentsia; his tragic assassination; and last, but not least, the considerable amount of Kennedy wealth and influence invested in the creation of the myth. This helps explain why polls still often show him to be one of the two or three most admired American presidents.

—Kennedy was painted as a World War II hero for his actions as skipper of the PT-109. During a naval battle a Japanese destroyer rammed it, cutting it in half. Two men were killed, and though Kennedy's back was injured he swam for five hours, pulling another crewman to safety on a nearby island. A book and a movie were made about the event. Many historians, including Gary Wills, now wonder how Kennedy managed to escape court-martial for the PT-109 incident. The ramming did not occur during battle, as Kennedy had claimed, but during a lull when everyone on board was napping, possibly intoxicated. A fast, highly maneuverable PT boat could never have been rammed by a destroyer had the crew not been negligent.

—After being elected to the Senate, Kennedy required surgery on his back and, while recuperating, was supposed to have written *Profiles in Courage*, an account of United States senators who had risked their careers to do the right thing. It won the 1957 Pulitzer

Prize and helped establish Kennedy as a serious thinker. Few historians now believe that Kennedy had much to do with the writing of the book. Credit is usually given to Theodore Sorensen, the accomplished author who wrote speeches for Kennedy.

—Many people believe that at 43 years old, Kennedy was our youngest President. He was the youngest ever *elected*, but Theodore Roosevelt ascended to the office at age 42 after the 1901 assassination of William McKinley.

—Kennedy is generally numbered among liberal icons, but he was no kind of liberal we would recognize today. In 1954, Kennedy was the only Democratic senator who did not vote to censure Joseph McCarthy. Supporters point out he was in the hospital at the time; critics suggest he went out of his way to avoid condemning McCarthy, a friend of his father. As President, he lowered individual and corporate income taxes. He dragged his feet on civil rights, reluctant to alienate southerners in Congress, and through his Attorney-General brother, Bobby, had Martin Luther King Jr.'s telephone tapped. He was a hard-line Cold

Scene from PT-109 (1963).

Warrior who escalated the Vietnam War, launched the botched invasion of Cuba at the Bay of Pigs and approved subsequent CIA attempts to assassinate Fidel Castro.

LAUNCHING NUCLEAR WASTE INTO THE SUN WOULD BE A GOOD WAY TO GET RID OF IT

An ideal solution to the intractable problem of nuclear waste would seem to be launching it into the sun. Most people would assume that a waste-laden rocket could be fired through earth's gravitational field toward the sun, and that it then would be captured by the sun's gravity and be pulled to its doom. Actually, the whole mess would simply pick up the Earth's own orbital speed of 66,500 mph and go into its own orbit around the sun, never falling into that cosmic fusion reactor. It would be far easier to launch a rocket into interstellar space 3.7 billion miles away than to try to send it the 93 million miles to the sun. Of course, it might come back marked "Return to Sender."

A LEG FALLS ASLEEP BECAUSE ITS BLOOD SUPPLY IS CUT OFF

When a limb has been kept in an awkward position for too long, a feeling of numbness results, often attributed to a cutoff of the blood supply. This is followed by a "pins and needles" sensation as the blood seems to rush back in.

In fact, the phenomenon has nothing to do with blood flow, which continues normally. Numbness occurs when a major nerve gets compressed against a bone or hard external object. In the arm it is usually the ulnar nerve; in the leg, the peroneal nerve.

LEMMINGS COMMIT MASS SUICIDE BY PLUNGING OFF CLIFFS

Lemmings are one of those creatures whose behavior provides a useful metaphor for the inexplicable things that humans do (see "The Ostrich Hides Its Head in the Sand"). In the case of the lemmings, they are supposed to get together in great hordes periodically and march off cliffs into the sea. This mad suicidal urge has been compared to everything from the nuclear arms buildup to the tendency of people to slavishly follow fashion dictates.

Lemmings are cute, furry little rodents that live in Arctic regions. Every four or five years there is a "lemming year" in which their population explodes. Normally you might hardly see a lemming, but during these periods of exponential growth they're all over the place. In one such year near Hardanger, Norway, the lemming population, normally around 22,000, mushroomed to 125 million. It became almost impossible to travel by car or train, as the roads and rails were greased with the guts of squashed lemmings. Naturally, with this level of crowding, hordes of the critters head off in search of green pastures and a little elbow room. If their migrations bring them to the edge of one of those fjords, it's understandable that a bunch of them could fall off the edge, pushed by the masses behind them like fans at a Brazilian soccer match. This isn't suicide, though—just an accident. An animal programmed with a death wish wouldn't make evolutionary sense.

According to Joel Achenbach's *Why Things Are*, the suicide image was given a boost by those gentle folks who do Disney nature films. The 1958 documentary *White Wilderness* dramatically showed lemmings hurling themselves off a cliff to their deaths. It was a great scene, but in order to film it the production team went to a lot of trouble. Hundreds of the harmless little fuzzballs were captured, shipped to the filming location and herded off a cliff for the cameras. The publicity book for the movie explains the dramatic scene: "The dramatic pageant reveals the greatest mystery of the northland: the 'suicidal' migration of the lemming. Countless multitudes of the little furry creatures go headlong into the sea, over every obstacle, in a blind and pitiable frenzy induced by overcrowding."

Yeah, and a couple of shrieking assistant directors poking them with cattle prods.

LENIN SAID, "THE CAPITALISTS WILL SELL US THE ROPE WITH WHICH TO HANG THEM"

This punchy piece of political commentary is probably the most widely quoted utterance of Vladimir Ilyich Lenin, but scholars have never located the observation in his writings or in any record of his remarks. The closest thing they could find was the following:

"They [capitalists] will furnish credits which will serve us for the support of the Communist Party in their countries and, by supplying us materials and technical equipment which we lack, will restore our military industry necessary for our future attacks against our suppliers. To put it in other words, they will work on the preparation of their own suicide."

Whoever came up with the misquote has a good feel for the memorable phrase. Lenin did not. His well-known description of communist sympathizers as "useful idiots of the West" is also spurious. It was probably made up by anti-communists, who quote it frequently.

LEO DUROCHER SAID, "NICE GUYS FINISH LAST"

As manager of the league-leading 1946 Brooklyn Dodgers, Leo Durocher is supposed to have contemptuously dismissed the New York Giants with this pithy remark. It's not really what he said, though. During a bull session with sportswriters, at the end of a tirade against so-called "nice guys," Durocher waved toward the Giants' dugout and said, "The nice guys are all over there. In seventh place." Frank Graham of New York's *Journal-American* wrote up the tirade under the headline "LEO DOESN'T LIKE NICE GUYS." When the article was reprinted in *Baseball Digest*, "seventh place" was changed to "last place." As the remark was repeated it evolved into the shortened, punchy version.

For years Durocher protested that he had never made the remark as it was attributed to him. It didn't matter. It was one of those things that needed to be said, and it needed a suitable curmudgeon as author. The irascible Durocher was ideal, so the paternity was his whether he wanted it or not.

Eventually Durocher stopped protesting—he must have realized that the misquote had given him an immortality far beyond the realm of sports. He even used it as the title of his 1975 autobiography.

THE LIBERTY BELL WAS RUNG WHEN THE DECLARATION OF INDEPENDENCE WAS SIGNED, CRACKING IT

It is true that the Liberty Bell hung in Philadelphia's Independence Hall at the time the Declaration of Independence was signed. It is also inscribed with the message "Proclaim Liberty throughout all the Land unto all the Inhabitants Thereof." Outside of that, what exactly has made it one of America's most sacred patriotic symbols?

—It was supposedly rung to celebrate the signing of the Declaration of Independence, but there's nothing to support that belief. John Adams reported that the bells in Christ Church rang out, but doesn't say anything about the bell in the building he was in, which you'd figure he would have noticed.

—Its famous crack had nothing to do with any excessive pealing on Independence Day. The bell developed a crack as soon as it was tested upon its arrival at Philadelphia in 1753. It had to be recast twice. The large crack it still carries didn't occur until 1835, when it was tolling for the funeral of Chief Justice John Marshall.

—Its dramatic inscription does not refer to liberty of the sort that the American Revolution was fought over, obviously, since it was cast in London. The name "Liberty Bell" was bestowed upon it in 1839 by abolitionists, and they were thinking of liberty for slaves, not for the colonists.

The Liberty Bell did not become a major patriotic symbol until 1847, when George Lippard indulged in a little creative writing about its role in the Revolution in his *Legends of the American Revolution*. This marked the first appearance of the story that "an old man with white hair and sunburnt face" rang the bell to celebrate the signing, while "a flaxen-haired boy with laughing eyes of summer blue" watched at his side. After the publication of this fairy tale, the bell began to be regarded as one of our patriotic symbols. Before that the bell had had no particular mystique. Philadelphia had even tried to sell it for scrap in 1828. There were no takers.

LIE DETECTORS DETERMINE IF SOMEONE IS LYING

The Chinese used to employ an ingenious system to determine if a criminal suspect was lying. They filled his mouth with uncooked rice and ordered him to spit it out. If he was nervous, his mouth would tend to be dry and little of the rice would stick inside. On this basis his guilt might be decided. We've come a long way since then—we have the lie detector, a gadget with lots of straps and wires that charts a subject's blood pressure, pulse rate, respiration and galvanic skin reflex simultaneously as he answers questions. The interrogator looks for physiological changes as clues that the subject may be lying, under the theory that he will not be able to control his involuntary responses to stress. It's a lot more impressive than uncooked rice, but may not work any better.

The lie detector, or polygraph, is more of a nervousness detector than a lie detector. Its supporters claim accuracy rates of as high as 95% in the hands of a skilled operator, but detractors point out that that is only true when the device is used on criminal suspects against whom strong evidence already exists. It can be a useful tool in the

hands of a skilled interrogator, especially when the subject is intimidated by the equipment—some criminals break down and confess during polygraph sessions. However, when used indiscriminately on populations, including many innocent parties, its reliability plummets. When applied wholesale to root out pilfering employees or leaking government bureaucrats it may identify the guilty—but it also usually incorrectly identifies as guilty many who are innocent. When lie detector tests were administered to White House officials to find the source of leaks during the Reagan administration, national security adviser Robert McFarlane was pinpointed. He protested his innocence, was polygraphed again and failed the second time as well. With his job in jeopardy, McFarlane prevailed upon *New York Times* reporters to tell Reagan that he was not the source of the leaks. Without naming their sources they did clear McFarlane. The lie detector had been wrong. Perhaps the actual leaker had learned the art of beating the polygraph—it's not that hard. Tricks as simple as biting your tongue or pressing down on a tack hidden in your shoe can produce false readings of stress. In the Whitewater case, much was made of the fact that Hillary Rodham Clinton's chief of staff, Maggie Williams, had passed a lie detector test. These tests were administered by sympathetic examiners, though, and she had been allowed several practice runs. That would render the results meaningless.

The use of lie detectors has been banned in the workplace and lie detector results are not admissible as evidence in federal court or in most state courts.

LIGHTNING NEVER STRIKES IN THE SAME SPOT TWICE, ETC.

The old adage that lightning never strikes in the same spot twice is probably meant to be taken figuratively; literally, it couldn't be more wrong. Lightning follows the path of least resistance and is *more* likely to strike the same spot over and over. New York's World Trade Center towers are hit dozens of times a year.

We usually think of lightning striking from the clouds to the earth, but tall buildings and mountaintops often initiate lightning that strikes upward to the clouds. Since lightning travels at 100,000 miles a second, it's hard to keep track of its direction.

In *Back to the Future*, the mad scientist uses lightning to jumpstart the time machine in his DeLorean—there was nothing else that could provide the necessary power. It is true that a lightning flash can unleash 100 million volts, more than could be produced in that instant by all the generators in the United States combined. That's not as much power as you'd expect, though. The flash is so brief—as little as a millionth of a second—that all its power would only run a lightbulb for a month or so.

Nearly 100 people are killed by lightning in an average year, more than are usually killed by tornadoes, hurricanes, ice storms, flash floods or blizzards. Nevertheless, lightning is not that good at killing those it strikes. Every year, 70 to 80% of people struck survive. Speaking of lightning striking the same place more than once, the *Guinness Book of Records* tells of park ranger Roy C. Sullivan of Virginia, who was struck by lightning seven different times over a thirty-five year period. On different occasions he lost a toenail, burned off his eyebrows and hair, and was hospitalized with minor burns. He earned the nickname "the human lightning rod." (He eventually killed himself over an unrelated romantic matter.)

"LIGHTS, CAMERA, ACTION!" SHOUTS THE DIRECTOR

Think that's what the director yells when it's time for Schwarzenegger to steel his gaze and cut loose with his belt-fed

M-60? They haven't said it in Hollywood since Arnold was in lederhosen. The directive dates from the days when illumination was supplied by carbon-arc lights, which required considerable adjustment and attention and had to be turned off regularly to cool. Before the cameras rolled, the director had to be sure that they were working properly. The gas-induction globes (or HMIs) now in use can be pretty much taken for granted. Recording equipment takes a moment to "come up to speed" for accurate sound quality, so the current command is generally, "Roll sound. Roll camera. Action!"

Incidentally, it is the assistant director who issues the first two orders; only the director calls for the action.

LINCOLN WAS POOR; USED THE NICKNAME "ABE"; WROTE THE GETTYSBURG ADDRESS ON THE BACK OF AN ENVELOPE

—Lincoln may have been born poor, but that's judging by the standards of today. In fact, one historian has pointed out that his father belonged to the top 15% of taxpayers in his community. Regardless of how poor he started out, he didn't remain that way—a few years into his legal practice in Springfield, Illinois, he was earning $1,200 to $1,500 a year—more than the governor. He was a lobbyist and corporate lawyer for the Illinois Central Railroad, and well-connected to the state's power structure. His wife, Mary Todd Lincoln, was from a wealthy family and part of the Springfield's social aristocracy.

—Lincoln signed his letters "A. Lincoln," and his wife Mary referred to him as "Mr. Lincoln" or "Father." He loathed the nickname "Abe." (Theodore Roosevelt likewise hated the nickname "Teddy," much preferring "T.R.")

—Lincoln supposedly scribbled out the Gettysburg Address on the back of an envelope while riding the train to Gettysburg. It is strangely satisfying to think that this rhetorical masterpiece could have been dashed off in a flash of inspiration, but such was not the case. Lincoln began working on the speech two weeks ahead of time, and there exist five drafts written on White House stationery.

LINDBERGH WAS THE FIRST TO FLY NONSTOP ACROSS THE ATLANTIC

Charles Lindbergh's *Spirit of St. Louis* touched down at Paris' Le Bourget Airport on May 21, 1927, after a 33 1/2 hour flight from New York. From that day on, he was an American hero like none other. Not only did he receive a $25,000 award, a ticker tape parade in New York and the Congressional Medal of Honor, but he was elevated to the status of an icon, the symbol of rugged American individualism.

Individualism is the key word here, because Lindbergh was not the first to fly across the Atlantic—he was only the first to fly across *alone*. The first nonstop flight across the Atlantic was made in 1919 by the team of William Alcock and Arthur Brown. They flew from Newfoundland to Ireland, a route which at 2,000 miles was 1,400 less

than the one Lindbergh took. There were two earlier dirigible crossings of the Atlantic as well, transporting a total of 64 passengers, so actually Lindbergh was the 67th to make the trip. Why was such a fuss made over Lindbergh? Granted, the solo flight was no picnic, but the key to Lindbergh's mystique was that he made such a perfect hero. Tall, rangy and handsome, confident but laconic, he might have been sent by central casting.

THE LION IS THE KING OF BEASTS; KING OF THE JUNGLE; ALWAYS LIONHEARTED

—Though the lion carries the rep of being the King of Beasts, it is not even the biggest of the big cats. A lion may be 6 to 8 feet long, 3 feet high at the shoulder, and weigh 400 to 500 pounds. The Siberian tiger, on the other hand, can be a foot longer, several inches taller and weigh up to 800 pounds. Even in its domain, the king does not always rule. Mature elephants and rhinoceroses can stomp a lion to death, and a herd of Cape buffalo can fend off lions without much trouble.

—Contrary to Tarzan movies, lions are not found in the jungle, if by jungle you mean a dense, tropical rain forest. They are found

mainly in the savanna, the open bush and grassy plains which cover much of Africa, and which are populated with the herds of grazing animals on which the lion feeds. To be perfectly correct, though, the word jungle is an Anglicization of a Hindi word which originally meant any sort of wilderness, including not only grasslands but deserts.

—Despite the lion's reputation for bravery, researchers in Tanzania have found that any pride of lions contains its cowards as well as its heroes. When one group of lions is challenged by another, there are some lions that will only fight if the odds are strongly in their favor, and others who won't fight under any circum-

Disney Productions

stances. According to the researchers, the lions who refuse to fight are nevertheless tolerated by the others.

LIVE TOGETHER FOR SEVEN YEARS AND YOU'RE LEGALLY MARRIED

Couples who have lived together for a decade or two without deciding whether or not they're ready for marriage are often told not to worry about it—after seven years, they were legally married anyway.

This notion seems to be mixed up with the practice of common-law marriage. A common-law marriage occurs between couples who agree to live together as if they were married and between whom there is no bar to legal marriage, such as one party being underage, having a preexisting marriage or being a farm animal. The seven-year figure has nothing to do with it, for better or worse.

LIZZIE BORDEN KILLED HER PARENTS WITH AN AX

Lizzie Borden would no longer be remembered if it weren't for that memorable ditty:

Lizzie Borden took an ax
And gave her father forty whacks
When she saw what she had done
She gave her mother forty-one.

And so Lizzie is enshrined in history as an ax murderer, helping women meet their quota among America's best-loved homicidal maniacs.

After Ms. Borden's parents were hacked to death in 1892, their spinster daughter became the prime suspect in a trial that was the O.J. case of its day. While the case was being tried, children began chanting the famous refrain. What's usually forgotten is that Lizzie was acquitted by a jury after only 66 minutes of deliberation. The most likely suspect, according to those who have studied the case, was—as anyone who reads Agatha Christie could have told them—the maid. (Apparently the family couldn't afford a butler.)

Lizzie was never able to live down that jingle, despite a life devoted to charity contributions and volunteer work. In her will she left a hefty stipend to see to it that her parents' graves were well cared for.

LOS ANGELES IS THE LARGEST AMERICAN CITY

Sometimes described as 17 small towns in search of a city, L.A.'s borders seem to stretch *ad infinitum*. Those visiting from the East Coast are often amazed to discover that a trip across town can be a matter of hours, even on the vast web of interconnecting freeways. Nevertheless, even at 464 square miles Los Angeles is not America's largest city—or even number two. The largest is Juneau, Alaska, whose 3,108 square miles offer plenty of personal space for its population of under 30,000. Anchorage is 1,732 square miles, though with a population of around 230,000, it's a lot more crowded. Jacksonville, Florida, covers 841 square miles and Oklahoma City, 604. Among cities with a population of at least 100,000, Los Angeles is number four, though it takes a backseat to no one in cosmic significance.

Gertrude Stein's famous put-down—"There's no *there* there"—is often mistakenly believed to have been directed at L.A. Actually, she said it about Oakland.

LYNDON JOHNSON SAID, "GERRY FORD IS SO DUMB HE CAN'T WALK AND CHEW GUM AT THE SAME TIME"

Lyndon Johnson's famous put-down of then-Republican Minority Leader Gerald Ford was cleaned up a little for public consumption; he actually said that the two actions Ford couldn't perform simultaneously were *farting* and chewing gum.

MAGELLAN WAS THE FIRST TO CIRCUMNAVIGATE THE EARTH

Most people think of Magellan as the first captain to circle the globe in a single trip, but he did not. On August 10, 1519, Ferdinand Magellan, a Portuguese captain in the service of Spain, set out from Seville with five ships and a crew of 250. He intended to complete Columbus' quest—to reach the Spice Islands of the East by sailing west. After three years of bitter weather, uncharted seas, a violent mutiny and starvation, one of his ships, the *Victoria*, arrived back at Seville with a surviving crew of 18. They were the first to successfully circumnavigate the earth. Magellan was not among them. In hand-to-hand fighting with the natives of Mactan Island in the Philippines; he had died facedown in the surf, stuck full of spears.

MAMA CASS CHOKED TO DEATH ON A HAM SANDWICH

Many rock stars have suffered from substance abuse, and in the case of Cass Elliot of the Mamas and the Papas that substance was food. When the 33-year-old singer died in London on July 27, 1974, initial reports were that she had choked to death on a ham sandwich. A week later, the coroner reported that Cass—who weighed 220 pounds at the time of her death—had died of a heart attack. There was no ham sandwich or food of any kind blocking her throat, and no drugs or alcohol in her blood. Nevertheless the image of the ham sandwich stuck, perhaps in innocent contrast to those rockers who have choked on their own vomit, or worse yet (to quote *This Is Spinal Tap*), on someone else's.

MAN IS THE ONLY ANIMAL THAT KILLS FOR SPORT

This is one of those statements insisting that not only are we not superior to other animals, we are actually *inferior* to them, our behavior being beneath that which would be expected of an animal. Anyone who's seen an episode of *The Jenny Jones Show* would find it hard to argue with this general proposition, but applied to sport hunting it is a bit unfair. The assumption is that when an animal kills, it kills in order to eat, while men hunt for the sheer, perverse enjoyment of it, even if they do eat what they kill. This proposition is hard to defend. A dog that kills a rabbit or a cat that kills a bird may have no intention of eating it—they kill, like the human hunter, because as predators they have a killing instinct. Any farmer whose henhouse has been visited by a weasel knows that the weasel was not just interested in a meal; while eating only one or two of the chickens, it will kill the rest of them in a mad frenzy. A Time-Life video on predators shows killer whales taking a seal from a beach and tossing it back and forth between themselves for amusement before killing it. Lions have been known to go on killing binges even when they are already gorged with food. Col. Jeff Cooper, a writer who has traveled and hunted extensively in Africa, says that a lion closing its teeth around the neck of an antelope displays the same expression of blissful release as it does at the moment of sexual climax. According to Cooper, the big cats don't kill in order to eat—they don't think that far ahead. They kill because they are genetically programmed to enjoy the act of killing itself. The meal is a bonus.

Similar pronouncements that place human behavior outside of that associated with animals include "Man is the only animal that makes war" and "Man is the only animal that kills his own kind." Neither of these propositions holds up. Ants make war, as do chimpanzees defending their turf. Wherever there are large populations of pack-hunting carnivores competing for the same territory, "wars" may occur between rival packs. Groups of hyenas in Tanzania's Ngoro-Ngoro region have been observed battling with a bellicose intensity to match any fractious European ethnic groups. As far as the second proposition, many animals routinely kill their own kind. The leading cause of death of male lions in the Serengeti is attack by other male lions.

However much we may like to think that civilization has changed us, human beings are still animals programmed with the instincts that got us through thousands of years of hunting and gathering, even if we now choose to express them in the boardroom or the racquetball court.

MARCO POLO BROUGHT SPAGHETTI FROM CHINA TO ITALY

When the Italian adventurer Marco Polo traveled to China in the fourteenth century, according to legend, he was amazed to find the Chinese eating lo mein; he brought the marvelous noodle back to Italy, where it became spaghetti. According to master debunker Tom Burnham, this story first appeared in 1929 in a trade magazine, *The Macaroni Journal*. It was an obvious spoof, describing Marco Polo taking dried pasta back with him, only to be unable to eat it until a sailor told him it had to be boiled first. What was the sailor's name? Spaghetti, and quite a coincidence too, as *spaghetti* means "string" or "cord" in Italian. The story took on a life of its own and was included in the 1939 film *The Adventures of Marco Polo*, in which Gary Cooper, in the featured role, slips some dried pasta in a small drawstring bag he kept for special treasures.

In his account of his travels Marco Polo wrote that the Chinese ate a form of pasta, but it didn't seem to strike him as unusual. Pasta has been around almost as long as wheat and was eaten by the Egyptians, Greeks and ancient Romans. Of course, they had to eat it without tomato sauce. The tomato was not known in Europe until it was brought over from Mexico in 1522.

MARIE ANTOINETTE SAID, "LET THEM EAT CAKE"

We all remember that Marie Antoinette tossed off this callous phrase when she was told that the peasants didn't have bread to eat. That was just the sort of insensitivity that the guillotine was intended to discourage.

As a matter of fact, she said nothing of the sort. The line comes from Rousseau's 1766 opus *Confessions*, where it is attributed to an unnamed "grande princesse." According to Rousseau, the remark was made around 1740, 15 years before the future queen of France was born. Marie Antoinette was not known for saying clever things, even nasty clever things, so "Let them eat cake" wouldn't have been like her.

Ms. Antoinette has more than one historical connection with the topic of pastry. An Austrian princess, she brought the croissant from the bakeries of Vienna to the patisseries of Paris.

MARIJUANA LEADS TO HARDER DRUGS

Most people who are addicted to cocaine or heroin began their drug involvement with marijuana, enabling advocates of total drug prohibition to argue that marijuana inevitably leads to the use of harder drugs. This logical fallacy has a Latin name: *post hoc, ergo propter hoc*—"after this, therefore because of this." The fact that one event follows another does not automatically prove that the former caused the latter. After all, most cocaine and heroin addicts started out on mother's milk. It's only logical that someone interested in using drugs would begin with marijuana—for years it was the cheapest and most commonly available drug. Some who use it may go on to harder drugs, some may continue to use it alone and others may stop using illegal drugs altogether and spend their money at the liquor store.

MARTIN LUTHER KING JR. WOULD HAVE OPPOSED AFFIRMATIVE ACTION

Martin Luther King Jr.'s plea that blacks be judged "not by the color of our skin, but the content of our character" has been used by conservatives to ally him in their effort to undo affirmative action. The implication is that King himself would have objected to race-based preferences. But in a January 1965 interview with *Playboy*, King was asked, "Do you feel it's fair to request a multibillion-dollar program of preferential treatment for the Negro, or for any minority group?"

King replied, "I do indeed."

MATTRESS TAGS: DO NOT
REMOVE UNDER PENALTY OF THE LAW

Go to any landfill and you'll see mattresses moldering away, their warning tags still inviolate. "Not to be removed under penalty of law," they say, and we do not, proving that we remain a law-abiding nation.

Maybe you're not like other people, though. When driving home at 4 A.M., you stop at red lights only long enough to check for patrol cars. You photocopy books in flagrant violation of the copyright laws. You don't always rewind your videocassettes before returning them. So, on an impulse, you tear off that tag. What business is it of the government what you do in the privacy of your own bedroom? Dammit, you're an American! But then the dread sets in. This isn't a momentary risk, like running a red light. An old mattress isn't so easy to get rid of. If you leave it in front of your house to be picked up with the trash, its tag conspicuously absent, it may attract the attention of some obscure regulatory agency with a SWAT team.

Fear not! This is one area of personal freedom that big government still allows us. The mattress tag admonition applies only to the retailer and is intended for the protection of the consumer. Once you buy your mattress, you may do with it what you will.

MEAT: TOP GRADE, GRADE A,
U.S. FINEST AND A-1 ARE THE BEST

Although meats are inspected and graded by the U.S. Department of Agriculture, the designations Top Grade, Grade A, U.S. Finest and A-1 are meaningless sell words employed by the supermarket. They carry no more authority than "taste tempting," "mouth watering," or "finger-licking good."

The government's rating system for meat uses eight official grades: Prime, Choice, Good, Standard, Commercial, Utility, Cutter and Canner, based largely on the meat's fat content. Your mouth's probably watering at the prospect of broiling up some of that Utility Grade steak.

MIAs—MORE IN VIETNAM THAN EVER BEFORE

Many veterans of the Vietnam War believe that large numbers of American servicemen declared "missing in action" were callously abandoned when the United States pulled out. Far from going away, the issue seems to be hotter than ever, as evidenced by the ubiquitous flags, decals and bumperstickers featuring the MIA emblem, as

well as movies such as *Uncommon Valor*, *Missing in Action* (Parts I & II) and, of course, *Rambo*. This concern is the main reason that it took so long to resume diplomatic relations with Vietnam.

Including those lost in Laos and Cambodia, the number of Vietnam War MIAs is put at 2,198 as of July 1995 and continues to go down as remains are returned and identified. Four to five hundred of these are pilots that disappeared over the ocean or otherwise went "off the scope," and are presumed dead. Only 55 are designated "last known alive." What rarely seems to come up in the discussion is that Vietnam produced significantly fewer MIAs than did other major wars. The number of MIAs from Korea is put at 8,100, and from World War II at 78,000.

The unique concern for the MIAs of the Vietnam War is due to the fact that, since we didn't win the war, we were never able to freely search battlefields or interrogate the enemy as we had after World War II. As an issue, it is symbolic of the war's inconclusiveness.

MICE LIKE CHEESE

A thousand cartoons have indoctrinated us with the impression that there is nothing a mouse craves more than cheese. In fact, there are any number of foods that mice prefer, including peanut butter, vegetables, meat and fresh fruit.

It's understandable. Most of us would also lose our taste for cheese if every time we nibbled on a piece, a metal bar came whizzing out of nowhere and snapped our necks.

MISSIONARY POSITION WAS TAUGHT
BY MISSIONARIES TO NATIVE PEOPLES

The term "missionary position" refers to face-to-face, man-on-top copulation. Legend has it was named after early missionaries who were shocked to encounter native peoples doing it dorsally (or "doggie style") and felt compelled to teach them the only position that was acceptable in the eyes of the Lord, should He happen to be watching.

There is no evidence supporting this story. There's nothing arcane about the missionary position—it's in the sexual repertoire of every culture on Earth. The expression itself, which we would expect to date from the nineteenth century, in fact did not show up until the 1960s, according to the *Oxford English Dictionary*. Coincidentally, this was about the same time as hippies began finding inspiration in Eastern wisdom, including some of the more startling insights of the Kama Sutra. They probably came up with the "missionary position" business to try to impress female hitchhikers they picked up in their VW buses.

Rumor has it that there is only one other land animal that mates face-to-face—the two-toed sloth.

MODERN, MECHANIZED
ARMIES ARE FASTER THAN EVER

In World War II, the Nazis utilized the *blitzkrieg*, a lightning-fast military strike that overwhelmed a country's defenses. Providing the speed were Germany's vaunted tanks. As fast as they were, today's tanks, capable of nearly 50 mph, would leave them in the dust. One would assume that armies move faster than ever, but that is not the case. The record for the fastest sustained daily advance

rate by an army has been unbroken after 700 years—it was set by the Mongols who swept across Asia and into Europe on horseback. The Mongols advanced 14 miles a day, something no modern army has been able to match. The modern, mechanized army is slowed down by its supply lines, but the Mongols' hardy steeds lived off the land, grazing wherever they happened to halt, even if they had to root around under snow for forage. Mongol warriors were equally adaptable—when they didn't have food available, they survived by opening a vein in their horses' necks and drinking a small amount of their blood. Each warrior took several extra horses as remounts so he could ride 24 hours a day, sleeping in the saddle if necessary. In one two-day period in 1221, Genghis Khan's army covered 130 miles. In a three-day period in 1241, the army covered 180 miles through deep snow.

It should be mentioned that in World War II, the Germans exaggerated the degree of their mechanization for propaganda purposes. They never had an adequate supply of motor vehicles, and to a large extent relied on horsepower. When Hitler invaded Russia in 1941, his army used 750,000 horse-drawn guns and vehicles along with about 600,000 motor vehicles. As for the Soviet Union, its army did not fully motorize its transportation until about 1960.

"MONEY IS THE ROOT OF ALL EVIL," IT SAYS IN THE BIBLE

If the Bible says that money is the root of all evil, what are we to do about it? Trade for stuff at some giant swap meet? Perhaps donate all we have to the nearest religious institution?

The actual words of (1 Tim 6:10) are "For the love of money is the root of all evil" [emphasis added]. Perhaps you still feel a bit guilty, suspecting that while you may not *love* money, your affection for it may border on the unseemly. Fear not, the good book has plenty of kindly things to say about it elsewhere. Try (Eccles. 10:19): "Bread is made for the feast, and wine gladdens life, but money answereth all things."

Even the idea that love of money is at the root of all evil doesn't hold up very well. People cause a great deal of trouble just for the hell of it.

THE MONGOOSE AND THE COBRA ARE SWORN ENEMIES

Thanks to "Rikki-Tikki-Tavi" in Rudyard Kipling's *The Jungle Book*, most of us think of the mongoose and the cobra as sworn enemies and know that when they go *mano a mano*, the mongoose always wins. The mongoose has no particular appetite for snake meat,

though—it'll kill and eat almost anything, including small rodents, birds and shellfish as well as eggs and fruit. One Indian species of mongoose eats nothing but crabs. Generally, the mongoose avoids the cobra, though it can usually—not always—overpower the slow-witted snake and break its back. Contrary to rumor, it enjoys no immunity to the cobra's venom. Against other kinds of snakes, the mongoose's chances drop off precipitously. In the West Indies, fights are sometimes staged between mongooses and pit vipers, and the smart money rides on the skinnier guys.

Yes, it's *mongooses*, not *mongeese*. The word *mongoose* has nothing to do with the word for those obnoxious, honking birds. It comes from *Manguso*, a bit of native argot the Brits picked up while imperializing India.

THE *MONITOR* AND THE *MERRIMAC* FOUGHT THE FIRST BATTLE OF THE IRONCLADS

The *Monitor* and the *Merrimac* are remembered as the Civil War ironclads that fought the four-hour Battle of Hampton Roads on March 9, 1862, an inconclusive engagement that marked the end of the age of wooden warships. It's handy that both their names began with the same letter—it makes them that much easier to recall. In fact, though, the Confederate ship the *Monitor* fought did not go by the name *Merrimac*.

Built in 1856, the *Merrimac* was a typical wooden United States Navy frigate. At the start of the Civil War it was docked in the Norfolk, Virginia, navy yard and was set on fire by retreating Union forces to keep it from falling into Southern hands. The Confederates salvaged it, cut away its upper hull and outfitted it with sloping armored sides. It was described as looking like "a floating barn roof." It was rechristened the *Virginia*, and it was under that name that it fought. The 1995 Civil War commemorative stamps put out by the U.S. Postal Service have attempted to clear the matter, correctly describing a depiction of the battle as being between the *Monitor* and the *Virginia*. Some say that the misnomer persisted so long because, at the time, Yankees felt the Rebels had no more right to rename a Northern vessel than they had to secede from the union.

Though the battle was a first, the idea of ironclad ships was not. In 1859 the French had launched the *Gloire*, which was covered in 4-inch-thick iron plates down to 6 feet below the waterline. Even earlier accounts exist, though their veracity is in doubt. The Koreans claim to have built an armored vessel in 1592. A Greek ship, the *Syracusa*, is supposed to have been plated with lead and have carried eight towers equipped with catapults, in addition to having saloons, a gymnasium, gardens, a temple and a pool. The huge ship, whose construction was supervised by Archimedes, was too large for the harbors of the day and ended up being given to Ptolemy of Alexandria as a curiosity.

MOSS GROWS THICKEST ON THE NORTH SIDE OF A TREE

Many of us hang onto this sort of wilderness lore figuring that it might come in handy if our plane crashes in that uncharted wilderness between Kennedy Airport and LAX. Keeping an eye on which side of the trees the moss grows, we would be able to make our way back to civilization, or at least the nearest McDonald's.

The logic behind this particular nugget is that the north side of a tree is the most shaded, and therefore most likely to harbor the dampness that moss requires. However, in a thick forest there is so much shade on all sides of a tree that there is no consistency to the pattern of moss growth. There are also so many other factors to consider—the lean of the tree, the water-holding properties of its bark, water runoff from nearby trees or the surrounding terrain, etc.— that no one short of Daniel Boone could safely hazard an opinion.

MOTHS EAT CLOTHES

It's not moths that eat your woolens and furs, it's moth larvae.

In nature, moths lay their eggs in the fur of dead animals. Trapped in your house, the moths seek out the next best thing— woolen clothes or any furs you've hidden away until this fuss about animal rights peters out.

Some species of moth don't eat anything at all. Moths lead brief lives. Their sole reason for being is to pay homage to the Porch-light God.

MUMMIES ARE PRODUCTS OF A SECRET EGYPTIAN ART OF EMBALMING THAT IS STILL NOT FULLY UNDERSTOOD

The Egyptians went to a lot of trouble to give their dead kings and queens a royal send-off. The brain was dissolved with special chemicals and then removed through the nose with metal hooks. The liver, lungs, stomach and intestines were removed. Salts were used to dry the corpse, which was covered in resins before being wrapped. When mummies were unwrapped 4,000 years later and found in a remarkable state of preservation, it was thought that the

Egyptians must have had secret, long-lost ways of preserving the dead. In fact, the dryness of the climate and the resulting lack of bacteria account for the lack of decomposition. Animals have been unearthed that died in the desert thousands of years ago and they were also well preserved, without all the folderol.

Belief in the mystic attributes of the mummies led to an unquiet afterlife for many of them. Mummies were brought back to Europe during the twelfth century, when "powdered mummy" was a popular medicine. Renaissance artists even mixed the powder into their paints, hoping the secret ingredients would preserve their colors.

MUSCLE TURNS TO FAT WHEN YOU NO LONGER EXERCISE

This old fallacy supplies a handy rationalization to those who don't exercise at all. Why spend four hours a day working out in a gym to look like Jean Claude van Damme or Cindy Crawford if, when you let up, you'll end up like John Goodman or Roseanne? Support for the theory seems to be supplied by all those fat guys who wear Gold's Gym T-shirts, and porky over-the-hill football stars that appear in Miller Lite commercials. Nevertheless, it cannot be. Muscle is muscle and fat is fat—one form of tissue cannot turn into the other. What is more likely is that those who are physically active may grow accustomed to indulging their appetite without putting on weight. When they're no longer burning off the calories, they start to pile on the pounds like everyone else.

A MUSHROOM CLOUD INDICATES A NUCLEAR EXPLOSION

No image is more identified with the atomic bomb than its ominous aftermath: the mushroom cloud. In fact, there is nothing uniquely atomic about the mushroom-shaped cloud—it occurs after any large above-ground explosion, including volcanic eruptions. It is formed when air displaced by a blast rushes back in and collides with itself. The smoke pushed to the center rises as the stem and then billows out to form the crown of the mushroom as the force is dissipated. Obviously, a nuclear explosion produces a bigger-than-average mushroom, and a decidedly poisonous one.

MUSSOLINI MADE THE TRAINS RUN ON TIME

Say what you will about fascism, but remember this—when you stepped out on that platform to catch the 8:02 to Naples, by golly it was there! Or so they say. According to Ashley Montagu's *The Prevalence of Nonsense*, there is no evidence that the Italian railroads took any greater notice of their published schedules between

1922 and 1945, the period of Mussolini's rule, than they did before or since. Those who wish to justify a government that imposed tyranny, tortured and imprisoned citizens, invaded Ethiopia and allied itself with Nazi Germany will have to look elsewhere.

NAPOLEON WAS SHORT

Hyper-aggressive little men who are driven to conquer the world in order to relieve their feelings of physical inadequacy are said to

have a Napoleonic complex. The expression assumes that that was Napoleon's problem, which is a little hard to understand since he was of average height for his time. Confusion arose because it was reported, after his autopsy, that he measured five foot two. In *Legends, Lies & Cherished Myths of World History*, Richard Shenkman writes that that measurement was based on the old French system of *pieds de roi*, which translates as a little over five foot six in our terms. The historian Michael Burns makes a different argument—that for most of his life Napoleon stood about five foot six, but shrank about three inches as he wasted away at the end. Burns points out that the height requirement for the French army at the time was four foot 11, and that hordes of aspiring soldiers were turned away for failing to meet it, so Napoleon was no shrimp among his contemporaries.

Too bad. Over the years, Napoleon's always been one of those great roles for short guys who do a good French accent. There's still Toulouse-Lautrec, though.

"NARC" IS A SLANG TERM OF THE SIXTIES

Back in the sixties, nothing could deflate your newly expanded consciousness faster than an encounter with a narc, an undercover officer working for the narcotics squad. The shorthand expression "narc" came to be applied as a noun and a verb to all squealers, snitches and informants.

The word actually has a longer history than most people would imagine, predating its association with narcotics. It's an old bit of thieves' slang, coming from the gypsy word *nak*, for "nose." In the criminal underworld, an informer is someone who has stuck his nose where it didn't belong.

NATHAN HALE'S LAST WORDS WERE "I ONLY REGRET THAT I HAVE BUT ONE LIFE TO LOSE FOR MY COUNTRY"

Nathan Hale, schoolteacher and spy for George Washington's army, is supposed to have defiantly declared as he stood on the scaffold, "I only regret that I have but one life to lose for my country." This heroic statement ranks among the greatest last words, and no doubt Nathan would have been proud to speak it, but we have no record that he did. A Yale graduate, he was probably familiar with the sentiment from Joseph Addison's 1713 tragedy *Cato*, which contains the line: "What pity is it that we can die but once to serve our country!"

Captain Frederick MacKenzie, a British officer who witnessed the hanging, wrote in his diary that the 21-year-old Hale "behaved with composure and resolution, saying he thought it the duty of every good officer to obey any orders given him by his commander-in-chief."

Not as memorable, but nothing like the sort of whimpering and sniveling we'd expect from kids today.

NECK RINGS STRETCH A WOMAN'S NECK

In certain primitive cultures, such as the Padaung of Burma, women wear stacks of brass rings around their necks, added one at a time from childhood. When the stack reaches 20 or so, the effect is that the neck has become stretched out nearly a foot. It appears that somehow the vertebrae have stretched or the ligaments between them have loosened. Using X rays, Dr. John M. Keshishian uncovered the truth for the June 1979 issue of *National Geographic*. What actually happens is that the collarbones are forced down and the ribs are bent sharply in a downward direction, creating the illusion of a longer neck.

The women who make this radical fashion statement are able to drink beverages only through straws, and their voices have been described as sounding as if they were speaking up the shaft of a well.

Don't laugh—it could be the next big thing.

"NEITHER RAIN NOR SNOW NOR HEAT NOR GLOOM OF NIGHT STAYS THESE COURIERS FROM THE SWIFT COMPLETION OF THEIR APPOINTED ROUNDS" IS THE OFFICIAL MOTTO OF THE U.S. POSTAL SERVICE

If your mail carrier takes the afternoon off with the appearance of the first snowflake, don't bother complaining on the basis of the well-known Postal Service motto. The Postal Service doesn't have a motto. The famous quote comes from the Greek historian Herodotus, dates from circa 500 B.C. and was written about the mounted postal couriers of ancient Persia. The architects who designed the New York City post office supplied it as the message to be inscribed along the top. It represents no guarantee, expressed or implied. It's probably the only laudatory quote anyone could dig up regarding mail service.

If those Persian mailmen didn't come through, you could probably slit them open and fill their bellies with fire ants. They weren't protected by a civil service contract.

NERO FIDDLED WHILE ROME BURNED

One of the more memorable characters of ancient Rome was the megalomaniac Emperor Nero, known for putting Rome to the torch so that he could rebuild the city to his own grandiose specifications. And then, while the city burned, Nero stood in a tower and played his fiddle, no doubt grinning fiendishly as the flames lit him from below.

Nero did fancy himself quite the *artiste*. Among the more horrendous atrocities he inflicted on his people were the plays and operas he wrote and performed, at which their attendance was compulsory. It has been suggested that Rome was burned because Nero fiddled, not the other way around. Actually, Nero's instrument of torture was the lyre. The fiddle wasn't invented for another 1,500 years.

Contrary to the tale, when the conflagration broke out, Emperor Nero was at his villa at Antium, 50 miles from Rome. He rushed back and directed the efforts to stop the blaze, which burned for over a week and consumed most of the city. He opened shelters for those who lost their homes, lowered the price of grain and had food brought in from the provinces. Nero actually behaved himself during the crisis, for one of the few times in his life. When his rebuilding project ran beyond schedule and over budget, though, he covered up by blaming the fire on the Christians, executing hundreds.

Whatever you may have heard, Nero did not feed Christians to the lions. There is no record of Romans feeding Christians to the lions at this or any other time, though they probably would have made an exception for Jim and Tammy Faye Bakker.

Nero, emperor of all Rome.

NIXON WAS A CONSERVATIVE PRESIDENT

To liberals, no politician came closer to representing the anti-Christ than did Richard Nixon. His anticommunist credentials were firmly established during the McCarthy period with his prosecution of the Alger Hiss spy case and his notorious 1950 senatorial campaign against Helen Douglas, whom he accused of being "pink down to her panties." As President, his right-wing reputation was maintained through his law-and-order stance and his continuance of the Vietnam War (which, in fairness, he did eventually bring to a close). But all in all, the Nixon presidency was far from conservative, as Tom Wicker pointed out in his book *One of Us*. Wicker described the many liberal causes Nixon espoused:

—He opened diplomatic relations with Communist China.

—He established the Environmental Protection Agency, the Occupational Safety & Health Administration, the Legal

117

Services Administration and the Equal Opportunity Commission. He more than doubled funding for the National Endowment of the Arts and National Endowment of Humanities, and vastly expanded the food-stamp program.

—It was he who gave us government-mandated racial quotas. Although Johnson had promoted a vague policy of affirmative action, it was the Nixon administration in 1970 that mandated goals and timetables under the Philadelphia Plan. It also extended civil rights legislation to women. Nixon supported the Equal Rights Amendment.

—In a speech delivered on February 18, 1971, he proposed a national health insurance plan that would have required businesses to pay 75% of the cost of employees' insurance, and an expansion of Medicaid to cover the working poor. Ironically, the plan was shot down by congressional liberals, who believed it didn't go far enough.

—His proposed Family Assistance Plan would have mandated a guaranteed annual income for poor families and would have extended government assistance to three times as many children as were covered by Aid for Families with Dependent Children payments.

Surprisingly, in terms of the legislation that he pushed, Nixon was probably the third most liberal President in American history, after Franklin Roosevelt and Lyndon Johnson. Carter and Clinton may have been more liberally inclined, but they got far less of the liberal agenda enacted.

NO SEX BEFORE THE BIG GAME

For years this was the admonition delivered by coaches to their athletes. It was assumed that sex the night before a major competition would sap a man's competitive edge. No such link has ever been proven, and as one coach, Darrell Royal of the University of Texas, dryly put it, "As a coach I spent most of my time concentrating on those activities I could control."

Those who still believe that sexual activity impairs an athlete's performance should consider two words: Wilt Chamberlain. The superstar basketball player wrote a revealing autobiography, *A View from Above*, whose title could be taken in more ways than one. Chamberlain estimates that he has had sex with about 20,000 different women since he was 15 years old, an average of 1.2 sex acts a day. Oddly enough, Chamberlain, who never went more than 20 hours without it, gives some credence to the "no sex" theory. It's just that he gives himself a lot of leeway on the cutoff point, writing that sexual encounters "were no-nos minutes before a game." (And presumably during half-time.) He chastises a Los Angeles Lakers player who was busted for soliciting two undercover policewomen posing as prostitutes a few hours before game time.

NORTH AND SOUTH POLES ARE THE COLDEST SPOTS ON EARTH

It seems logical to assume that as we progress northward, the climate gets progressively colder. Logical, but wrong. It might work if the surface of the earth were like that of a billiard ball, but there are a number of factors that influence climate besides the proximity to the poles, including ocean currents, mountains and prevailing winds. Due in part to ocean currents, Seattle is considerably warmer than East Coast cities on the same latitude. The mean temperature in January in Reykjavík, Iceland, is often the same as that in Milan, Italy. January's average temperature in Stockholm, Oslo or Helsinki is far milder than that of Minneapolis. Just seven miles from the equator in Africa, Mount Kenya is topped with a permanent glacier. Mount Chimboraza in the Andes of Ecuador is also close to the equator and also permanently snowcapped. You can be in the tropics and still freeze to death.

Temperatures at the North Pole are warmer on average than those in northern Siberia and central Greenland. The lowest temperature ever recorded was minus 126°F at Vostok, Antarctica, 900 miles north of the South Pole.

OCTOPUSES ARE DANGEROUS TO DIVERS

Somewhere in the human operating program it must be written that any creature with eight or more legs is up to no good. When those legs are covered with nasty-looking suction cups—*case closed*. Though most species of octopus are small, deep-sea varieties have been caught off the Alaskan coast that measured 32 feet from the tip of one tentacle to another. If such a creature got you in its vicelike grip, there would seem to be no escape. Victor Hugo described such an encounter in his 1866 novel, *The Toilers of the*

Sea. "What can be more horrible than to be clasped by those vicious thongs which adhere closely to the body by virtue of their many sharp points? But the wounds of these points is as nothing compared to that of the sucker discs. The points are the beast entering into your flesh. The discs are you, entering into the flesh of the monster."

The novel was a big hit and helped spread the octopus' fearsome reputation. Fortunately, despite their monstrous appearance, the eight-armed cephalopods are shy creatures that do their best to avoid divers. They spend most of their time hiding in holes and under rocks. On the occasions when they have wrapped a tentacle around a diver, the grip was easily dislodged. There are no recorded cases of an octopus attacking a diver.

"OH GIVE ME A HOME, WHERE THE BUFFALO ROAM, AND THE DEER AND THE ANTELOPE PLAY"

This western ballad contains two misnomers:

—The home where the buffalo roam is in Africa or Asia, the true buffalos being Africa's Cape buffalo and the water buffalo of Asia. What we have out West are more properly called bison, which differ from buffalo in having 14 pairs of ribs instead of 13, among other things. Bison are not exclusively American either. They crossed the Bering Strait land bridge to the Americas 500,000 years ago, and there are

still small herds of them in Poland and Russia.
—We do have deer in the American West, but no true antelope. What the song calls antelope is actually the pronghorn, the sole member of the family *Antilocapridae*. Antelopes grow their horns throughout their lives; pronghorns shed them annually.

It's too late to straighten any of this out—for one thing, it would ruin the meter of the song.

OLYMPIC GOLD MEDALS ARE GOLD
With all the revenues from those TV contracts, you'd think the Olympic committee could afford to give its star athletes something with some real class. In fact though, Olympic gold medals are actually gold-plated silver.
The real gold is in the commercial endorsements.

OPOSSUMS HANG FROM BRANCHES BY THEIR TAILS
The opossum has a prehensile tail which helps it balance when climbing trees, but it cannot hang by it.

THE OSTRICH HIDES ITS HEAD IN THE SAND
This image will never die, because it creates an image for which we have no suitable replacement. The stupid ostrich, faced with danger, sticks its head in the sand and, no longer able to see the threat, imagines itself safe. Just the thing to liken your opponent to if he's not facing up to the dangers of nuclear proliferation or second-hand smoke. The problem is that the ostrich does no such thing. Faced with danger it either runs away at speeds up to 40 mph or fights with its legs, whose powerful kicks can put a right-angle bend in an iron bar half an inch thick. Only humans are stupid enough to hide their heads in the sand.

How did the image arise? Sometimes the ostrich listens intently for sound with its head near the ground. Sometimes it lowers its head to rest its muscles. Sometimes it pokes its head into bushes, out of curiosity. While guarding its nest, it lays down with its neck flat along the ground. In this position it resembles a bush. But if it buried its head in the sand it would suffocate, and it's not that dumb.

OSWALD COULDN'T HAVE FIRED THREE TIMES

There are some people you can't win an argument with, among them Elvis fans, Islamic fundamentalists and Kennedy assassination conspiracy theorists. Nevertheless, there is one point often raised by that latter group that should be laid to rest—that no one has ever been able to place three shots as quickly and accurately as Lee Harvey Oswald supposedly did. If true, that fact alone is sufficient to destroy the lone gunman hypothesis.

Ironically, this belief was initially spread by the Warren Commission. Though it concluded that Oswald had acted alone, its own tests suggested otherwise. Three top-ranked marksmen were asked to match Oswald's feat: three shots at a moving target within the 5.6 second time established by the Zapruder film. (Most analysts now think that the Zapruder film ran slow, and that the actual time was slightly longer.) Only one was able to get off the shots in the allotted time, and none was able to hit the head or neck of a stationary target, let alone get two hits on a moving one as did Oswald. Conspiracist Mark Lane made much of this revelation in his best-selling book on the assassination, *Rush to Judgment*. Recently released intelligence reveals that Fidel Castro conducted his own tests to see if he could make the shots. Unable to do so, and considering himself a sharpshooter, Castro concluded that three shooters must have been involved. (Whether or not Castro is in fact a good marksman is probably not open to discussion in Cuba.)

In 1967 CBS News conducted a reenactment of the assassination scenario for a documentary special. It brought 11 volunteer marksmen to a mock-up of the Dealey Plaza site. A 60-foot tower with a window duplicated the vantage point of the sixth floor of the Texas Book Depository. Stretching down a slight grade beneath it was a track representing Elm Street. A small, electric vehicle ran along the track at 11 mph, the speed of Kennedy's limousine, with a target of a man's head and shoulders inside.

The shooters had no opportunity to practice for the challenge. None had even been given advance information as to why they were being brought to the range. Nevertheless, the marksmen averaged 5.6 seconds for their three shots, with two out of three hits on the target, duplicating Oswald's performance exactly. One put three holes within 3 inches in 4.8 seconds.

At the conclusion of the documentary, Walter Cronkite said,

"These points strengthen the Warren Report's basic finding. They significantly weaken a central contention of the critics—their contention that Oswald could not have done it because he did not have enough time to fire...Did Lee Harvey Oswald shoot the President? CBS News concludes that he did."

In his time, CBS anchor Walter Cronkite was dubbed "the most trusted man in America." Assassination conspiracists aren't the trusting kind, though.

OVERPOPULATION IS THE PRIMARY CAUSE OF STARVATION

The connection between overpopulation and starvation seems obvious, but on examination it falls apart. There are countries that are both crowded and malnourished, but there are more that are one but not the other. Japan, Hong Kong and Singapore are extremely densely populated, but do not suffer from any shortage of food. In fact, heavily industrialized Japan, where farmland is at a premium, nevertheless produces as much rice as Burma, which is twice as large and entirely rural, while France produces more wheat than Argentina and Australia combined. Meanwhile, Cuba, Honduras and Angola have food shortages but have plenty of arable land.

Food shortages have much more to do with the political organization (or lack of it) of a society than they do with overpopulation. In Honduras, multinational corporations own most of the arable land and use it to raise export crops. In Cuba, Castro imposes a communist-style agricultural system on his society, fearing that if farmers were allowed to freely market their food it would weaken his control. Some of the worst famines of the twentieth century were the result of deliberate political policies— 5 million starved in the Ukraine in the 1930s, and 30 million starved in China between 1958 and 1961, as Stalin and Mao sought to collectivize farming. Starvation in Somalia was due to the anarchic political situation rather than any shortage of food—rice donated by relief organizations was confiscated by gangs and sold in the market for a lower price than it was available anywhere else on Earth, but still out of reach of much of the population.

During the famine in Ethiopia in the mid-1980s, Western countries contributed vast amounts of food. Rock musicians held Food-Aid concerts and produced a hit song to raise funds for relief. The effort seemed to go for nothing—food rotted on the wharves as people continued to starve. It became clear that the Ethiopian government was using starvation to try to break the Eritrean insurgency. Perhaps harsher measures, such as broadcasting *We Are the World* nonstop over the radio, would have extracted concessions sooner.

OYSTERS ARE UNSAFE IN MONTHS WITHOUT AN *R*

Someone said that the bravest person who ever lived was the first one who ate a raw oyster. Suspicions linger about the slimy mollusk; for example, it has always been considered unsafe to eat an oyster in a month without the letter *r* in it—in other words, the summer months. This has nothing to do with oysters and lots to do with temperature. Before the widespread availability of refrigeration, there was a danger that, between May and August, oysters might have been stored at temperatures that allowed them to spoil.

Today there is no reason not to enjoy the phlegm-like delicacy any time of the year.

THE PANAMA CANAL TRAVELS EAST TO WEST FROM THE ATLANTIC TO THE PACIFIC

It would be logical to assume that when you pass through the Panama Canal from the Atlantic to the Pacific you would be traveling east to west. This is not true. Ships entering from Colon on the Atlantic coast travel due south 10 miles until they enter Gatun Lake. From there they reenter the canal and head southeast for the remaining 50 miles, leaving the canal more than 20 miles east of the point at which they entered.

Because of the crooked shape of the Panamanian isthmus, a Panamanian can watch the sun rise over the Pacific and set on the Atlantic.

PATRICK HENRY SAID, "GIVE ME LIBERTY OR GIVE ME DEATH"

Sometimes the task of debunker is a painful one, nevermore so than when examining America's patriotic lore. The more you delve into it, the more you discover that the proudest moments of our history may never have happened or did not happen the way we have been told. When a new nation comes into being, it needs to define itself quickly, and one of the ways it does so is by manufacturing tradition. Historian Daniel Boorstin describes early

Americans as a people "so hungry for resounding utterances that they relived their past in counterfeit orations."

Most of us remember Patrick Henry for the fiery speech he delivered to the second Virginia Convention in March 1775. It concluded with the stirring words: "Is life so dear or peace so sweet as to be purchased at the price of chains and slavery? Forbid it, Almighty God, I know not what course others may take, but as for me, give me liberty or give me death!"

Makes you want to grab your musket and go smoke some redcoats.

But was that what Patrick Henry really said? The speech was delivered without notes, and there is no contemporary record of it. Washington and Jefferson, who were present at the oration, did not mention it in their writings. The words come down to us from William Wirt, a biographer who "reconstructed" it some decades later on the basis of the recollections of two people who were present, John Tyler and St. George Tucker. Wirt was a florid writer, and many historians believe that the famous words owe more to the fuzzy recollection of Tyler and Tucker and the vivid imagination of Wirt than they do to Patrick Henry. To realize how unlikely it would be that anyone could recall Henry's actual words, try to recall any speech you may have heard only once, such as Patrick Buchanan's address to the 1992 Republican Convention. Let's see...something about looters in L.A., something about a religious war, something about cross-dressing Democrats...

PAUL REVERE RODE ALONE AND YELLED "THE BRITISH ARE COMING!"

Paul Revere was a leader of colonial opposition to the British, and one of the "Indians" at the Boston Tea Party. He participated in the Stamp Act Riots and served as a paid courier for the revolutionary forces. Despite these patriotic services, and his renown as a silversmith, Revere would probably have faded into obscurity if it weren't for Longfellow's poem "The Landlord's Tale: Paul Revere's Ride" (not "The Midnight Ride of Paul Revere," as it is sometimes called), probably the best-known poem in American historical literature. It begins:

Listen, my children, and you shall hear
Of the midnight ride of Paul Revere
On the eighteenth of April, in Seventy-five;
Hardly a man is now alive

125

Who remembers that famous day and year.

Hardly a man was then alive because Longfellow's poem was written 90 years after the fact, and Longfellow numbered among those whose recollection of the event was dim. The poem fails to mention the two others who rode with Paul Revere to warn of British troop movements—a cobbler named William Dawes and Samuel Prescott, a doctor. Dawes and Revere had already warned the Lexington area when, around midnight, they were joined by Prescott. The three set off to Concord but were spotted by a British patrol. Revere was captured and detained. Dawes headed back to Lexington. Prescott leaped a fence on his horse and brought the warning to Concord. It was Dr. Prescott who actually warned Concord's citizenry in time to save the stores of weapons and ammunition that supplied the "shots heard round the world" the next day at Concord. Paul Revere was released by the British, but without his horse, and had to return to Lexington on foot.

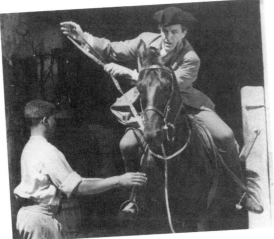

Though the poem doesn't mention what Paul Revere shouted by way of warning, it wasn't "The British are coming!" as we always hear, but rather "The regulars are out!", referring to British regular troops.

The ride on the night of April 18, 1775, was a rather minor incident at a time when many heroic events were taking place. No one would probably be more surprised than Paul Revere to know that it would make him one of the most celebrated figures of the American Revolution.

THE PEANUT IS THE MOST COMMON TYPE OF NUT

The peanut doesn't really belong to the nut family. It's actually a legume—as its name indicates, it's more of a pea than a nut. A lot of the other things you find in a can of mixed nuts don't belong there either. Neither the cashew, the almond, nor the Brazil nut is classified as a nut by botanists. The cashew is the seed of a plant related to poison ivy, and the almond is found inside the pit of a peach-like fruit. The Brazil nut is actually a type of fruit. Examples of true nuts include the walnut, pecan, chestnut, beechnut, hickory, acorn and filbert. True nuts generally grow on trees or in dysfunctional families.

PENNIES ARE COPPER; NICKELS ARE NICKEL

America's dimes, quarters, half dollars and silver dollars were silver until 1964, but when the silver in the coins became more valuable than their face value they were changed to nickel-covered copper. Time and inflation march on, and by 1982 it was no longer economical to mint pennies from copper. They had been 95% copper and 5% zinc; they were changed to zinc with a thin coating of copper. Where did all the copper go? It's in the nickels, which are now 75% copper and only 25% nickel.

THE PENNSYLVANIA DUTCH ARE IMMIGRANTS FROM HOLLAND

The people referred to as Pennsylvania Dutch have roots not in Holland but in Germany. "Dutch" is a loose translation of *Deutsch*, as in Deutschland, or Germany.

The people of Holland prefer to call themselves Netherlanders or Hollanders rather than Dutch. If you are aware of what the Germans did to Holland in World War II, you'll understand why they wish to keep their national identity distinct.

PEOPLE CAN BE SUCKED OUT OF AN AIRPLANE THROUGH A BROKEN WINDOW

At the climax of *Goldfinger*, James Bond is fighting Goldfinger in an airplane when a stray bullet shatters a window. The decompression sucks the portly villain through the small window like a vacuum sucks a hard-boiled egg into a wine bottle. In the 1970s, when there was a flurry of skyjackings, this image came to mind when it was suggested that armed guards be posted on airplanes. Many people assumed that a stray bullet that penetrated the shell of a pressurized aircraft could cause a calamity.

Actually, a small hole would make little difference to the pressure inside a jet. No passenger aircraft is airtight—the cabin is kept pressurized by continually pumping in air, which leaks out through any number of small cracks. Even if a window were shattered, the results would not be catastrophic. Doors have occasionally blown off passenger jets in flight without any injuries, though the planes had to descend to a lower altitude. On April 22, 1988, an Aloha Airlines Boeing 737 was cruising at 24,000 feet when a large section of its cabin skin tore off. The entire upper half of the plane was completely open for 18 feet of its length. One flight attendant was swept out, but the 89 passengers managed to remain in their seats, though after the plane landed none was able to recall how the in-flight movie ended.

"PIGS" WAS A SIXTIES EPITHET FOR THE POLICE

During the urban upheavals and student rebellions of the 1960s, police officers got accustomed to hearing themselves referred to as "pigs." Some tried to make the best of it, suggesting that the epithet was an acronym for Pride, Integrity, Guts and Service. Despite its association with the sixties, though, the use of the name *pigs* for policemen had been part of English and American underworld slang since the early nineteenth century.

PILGRIMS WERE THE FIRST EUROPEANS IN THE NEW WORLD; LANDED AT PLYMOUTH ROCK; LIVED IN LOG CABINS

—Those of us who think of the Pilgrims as the first permanent European settlers of the United States are forgetting about Jamestown, Virginia, settled in 1607. We're also guilty of Anglocentrism, if you need something new to feel guilty about. At the time the Pilgrims settled Massachusetts in 1620, the Spaniards had already been in St. Augustine, Florida, for 55 years. St. Augustine remains the oldest continually settled European-founded city in the United States. The Spanish outpost of Santa Fe predates the Plymouth settlement by 10 years. (Of course, the Pueblo Indian village of Acoma, New Mexico, was founded in around A.D. 975 and has been occupied to the present day.)

—The Pilgrims never called themselves that. As members of the English Separation Church, a radical faction of the Puritans, they referred to themselves as Separatists. It was two centuries after their arrival that the title Pilgrim Fathers was applied to them in a speech by Daniel Webster. Not everyone aboard the *Mayflower* was a Pilgrim either. Of the 102 passengers, only 40 or so could be identified as such.

—The *Mayflower*'s first landing was not at Plymouth Rock, but at Provincetown, on the tip of Cape Cod. While the *Mayflower* was moored in Provincetown's harbor, a small exploratory party set out in a small boat, landed at what is now Eastham and several days later arrived at Plymouth. There is no reason to believe that the party stepped off on Plymouth Rock. That detail was provided in 1741 by the octogenarian John Faunce, who was born 26 years after the landing. It was popularized at the bicentennial celebration of the landing in 1820.

—Picture the Pilgrims living in log cabins? They had no idea what a log cabin even looked like, having never seen one in England. Log cabins didn't appear in America until later in the 1600s when they were introduced by Swedish settlers along the Delaware River. Pilgrims first lived in tents and Indian-style wigwams, but soon set about building the sort of domiciles they were accustomed to—framed houses.

PING-PONG IS A CHINESE GAME

Because of its name, and because the Chinese seem to have a particular talent for it, many assume that Ping-Pong was invented in China. In fact, Ping-Pong was originated by British army officers stationed in India in the 1880s. Its real name is table tennis; Ping-Pong is the registered trademark of a company that makes table-tennis equipment. Like many other catchy product names—Kleenex, Xerox and Brillo—it has entered the language as a generic expression.

PIRANHAS TERRORIZE THOSE
WHO LIVE ALONG THE AMAZON

There are few creatures with as deadly a reputation as the piranha fish. If people enter piranha-infested waters, a churning mass of the fish will supposedly descend upon them, picking them to the bone in seconds.

The piranha is an intimidating-looking creature with, in the words of ichthyologist Dr. George S. Myers, "...teeth so sharp and jaws so strong that it can chop out a piece of flesh from a man...as neatly as a razor, or clip off a finger or toe, bone and all, with the dispatch of a meat cleaver." In a large group, they are perfectly capable of killing and consuming large animals. Nevertheless, an article in the November 1970 issue of *National Geographic* reveals that piranhas have a lot more to fear from people than people do from piranhas. Rather than inspiring terror among the people who live along the South American rivers they populate, they are valued as a major food source. People swim and wash clothes in piranha-infested waters with little concern, and routinely ford rivers with their cattle. Attacks occasionally occur, but they are not as common or as

deadly as many would assume; most bites are suffered by fishermen who are handling the piranhas they have caught. In two decades of roaming the outback of Brazil, anthropologist Harald Schultz met only seven persons who had been injured by piranhas. There is no documented case of a human having been killed and eaten by the fish. The myth of their unparalleled ferocity was spread by Theodore Roosevelt's 1914 book *Through the Brazilian Wilderness*. On his ill-fated exploration of the Amazon, a member of his party lost part of a foot to piranhas.

Piranhas can be quite dangerous to each other. When one is hooked on a fishing line, others may take advantage of its helplessness. Sometimes there is little left but its head when the fisherman reels it in. Their normal diet is smaller fish, insects, frogs, lizards and small mammals.

The natives of the Amazon worry far more about the stingray. It swings its sawtoothed spine with great force, leaving a painful wound that is slow to heal and usually becomes infected. In fact, stingrays are probably the most dangerous aquatic creatures, causing far more injuries than piranhas or sharks combined.

PIRATES MADE CAPTIVES WALK THE PLANK; FLEW THE SKULL AND CROSSBONES

In the early eighteenth century pirates prowled the seas, and an unfortunate sailor captured by them knew what lay in store. He would be blindfolded, have his arms tied and be prodded by cutlasses down the length of a plank extending off the side of their ship. As they roared their amusement he'd plunge into the depths, lunchmeat for the nearest shark.

Really? The vivid image of "walking the plank" did not exist before an 1887 *Harper's Monthly* illustration by pirate enthusiast Howard Pyle. There is only one account of such an occurrence, and it had nothing to do with pirates. In 1769, long after the pirates had been eradicated by the British navy, a seaman about to be hanged for his part in a mutiny revealed that he and his fellow mutineers had forced the loyal crewmen "to walk on a plank, extended from the ship's side, over the sea, into which they were turned, when at the extreme end." This is the only mention of the ritualistic use of a plank. Mediterranean pirates who preyed on Roman shipping around 100 B.C. played a similar game on their captives. When captured Romans identified their nationality in hopes of receiving better treatment, the pirates would feign awe, drop to

their knees, beg for mercy and tell the Romans that of course they were free "to walk home." The only place they could walk, of course, was over the rail and into the sea.

It appears that when the time came to get rid of annoying captives, no one bothered with a plank. They were simply tossed overboard.

The image of the skull and crossbones has become so familiar that you would think the pirates got together and voted on a standard design (then picked up some royalties when it was used on iodine bottles). Actually, since pirate flags were not available through mail order, every pirate vessel had its own fear-inspiring pennant that it raised when closing in on a victim. Variations on the skull-and-crossbones pattern were used, but also skeletons, crossed sabers, images of pirates, and arms wielding swords. Often the pennant wasn't black, but red; it has been suggested that the expression "Jolly Roger" comes from the French's ironic description of the pirate pennant as *joli rouge*, or "pretty red."

PLASTIC BAGS ARE WORSE THAN PAPER FOR THE ENVIRONMENT

When you get your groceries bagged, the clerk may ask you your preference—paper or plastic? Those who are conscientious about the environment generally pick the paper bag, figuring it's recyclable and biodegradable, but despite the stigma that plastic carries, paper may be the worse choice.

As John Luoma wrote in the March 1990 issue of *Audubon Magazine*, "As we all knew, plastics can be expected to last virtually forever in a landfill. But so, it seems, will most of the supposedly biodegradable things. Each nicely brown, seemingly earthy, Kraft paper bag chosen by the virtuous grocery shopper at the checkout line is in fact, at least as polluting, and probably more so, than the polyethylene (plastic) alternative."

In order to understand the relative merits of paper and plastic, it's necessary to do what in industry is termed a "life cycle analysis." A product has a life—from the amount of material and energy necessary to manufacture its raw material, to the energy necessary to manufacture the product, to the energy required to transport it, to its primary use, secondary use and eventual recycling or disposal. There's more to the plastic vs. paper debate than the fact that the plastic may linger longer when tossed along the roadside.

—Most paper bags are made from virgin paper, a process that costs trees, releases dioxin, contributes to acid rain and pollutes large volumes of water. It requires 40% less energy to produce the plastic bag, and the process produces 70% fewer atmospheric emissions and 94% less water pollution.

—Plastic bags are so much lighter and compact that they require far less energy to transport. It takes seven trucks to carry the number of paper bags that one truck could carry if they were plastic.

—The paper bag can be recycled, but not that efficiently—it has to be repulped, beginning the polluting process all over again. It takes 85 times as much energy to recycle paper as plastic on a per-pound basis, according to Dr. Frank N. Kelley, the Dean of Polymer Science and Engineering at the University of Akron .

—A large percentage of either type of bag will not be recycled, ending up in landfills. Here the lesser bulk of the plastic is again a plus—it creates 80% less solid waste. It may take hundreds of years to decompose, but in buried landfills this is equally true of paper. Thirty-five-year-old newspapers have been dug out of landfills that could still be read.

By most ecological criteria the plastic bag comes out significantly ahead of the paper, but both exact a cost on the environment. To be truly virtuous bring your own shopping bags to the store.

PLUTO IS THE FARTHEST PLANET FROM THE SUN

Not at the moment.

Pluto was the last planet identified and, at an average distance of 3,670,000,000 miles from the sun, is generally thought as the farthest one out there, millions of miles past Neptune. But in the course of its 248-year revolution around the sun, Pluto's elliptical orbit brings it inside of Neptune's path for a 20-year period. The latest crossover occurred in 1979, and until 1999 Pluto will be 56 million miles closer to the sun than Neptune.

Break out the sunblock, Plutonians.

POCAHONTAS SAVED THE LIFE OF HER ENGLISH LOVER, JOHN SMITH

The incident for which Pocahontas is the most famous—saving the life of John Smith by throwing her body over his as he was about to be beheaded by her tribe—probably never happened. *A True Relation of Such Occurrences and Accidents of Note as Hath Happened in Virginia*, Smith's original account of his adventures in the New World, never mentions it, despite the fact that it was written in 1608, only a year after the incident is supposed to have happened. You'd think a last-minute reprieve from execution would rate pretty high on anyone's list of "occurrences and accidents." Nevertheless, it was only in his 1624 volume, *The General History of Virginia*, that Smith brings it up. By this time Pocahontas had achieved considerable celebrity on her own, having been received at the British court after traveling to England in 1616 as the wife of John Rolfe, and the first American Indian convert to Christianity. Many historians suspect that Smith was trying to share her spotlight with his much-delayed recollection, especially since he had a history of telling highly embellished accounts of his adventures. Those who believe John Smith's story suggest that what he experienced was a ritualistic mock execution rather than any serious threat to his life. Such ceremonies were part of the initiation rites of young braves. If the Indians actually intended to chop off his head, it is unlikely that Pocahontas would have been allowed to interfere.

Disney managed to offend people on both ends of the political spectrum with its depiction of the Indian heroine. One columnist dubbed her "Politicallycorrectahontas" for her relentlessly righteous views, another said she looked like she was attired by "Frederick's of Chippewa." Native American activists also objected to the Barbie-like figure and attire, clearly aimed more at doll merchandising than authenticity. The real Pocahontas was only 11 or 12 years old at the time in question, and would have gone around almost naked. Rather than having a mane like a supermodel, she would have sported a punk look—the tribal custom was to shave the top and sides of the head, with a long, braided lock in back.

Due to the fact that her father, Chief Powhatan, had 100 wives, Pocahontas was not the precious only child that the Disney story implies. She had 20 half-brothers and 10 half-sisters, although she was a particular favorite of her father. He gave her the pet name Pocahontas, meaning "playful one"; her real name was Matoaka.

Of course, John Smith is the classic fake name. Judging by Pocahontas' age when John Smith struck up with her, Jay Leno suspects his real name was "Buttafuoco."

POISON IVY AND POISON OAK ARE SPREAD BY SCRATCHING

If you ever get a case of poison ivy or poison oak you're bound to hear that you shouldn't scratch it because that will spread it—especially if you break the blisters. Naturally, you can't help scratching the cursed stuff and have to accept further eruptions as punishment for your lack of self-control.

Scratching is not a particularly good idea, since it can lead to infection, but it doesn't spread the rash. The reason that other eruptions may flare up days after the first one is that different areas of skin display a different sensitivity to its irritating oil, urushiol, and may have received a different amount. The oil may also have remained on clothing or shoes and may be picked up by the skin later.

PORCUPINES THROW THEIR QUILLS

When a porcupine is threatened, it bristles and it may lash its tail back and forth, but it cannot throw its quills. The quills are extremely sharp, equipped with barbs and only loosely attached to the porcupine's skin, but as long as you don't brush up against the porcupine you won't get stuck. Which makes you wonder why porcupine pelts have never been fashioned into women's coats—they'd be the perfect revenge on the kind of creep that likes to rub up against women on a crowded bus.

PROHIBITION MADE IT ILLEGAL TO DRINK ALCOHOL; PROHIBITION ENDED IN 1933

Prohibition began in 1919, with the passage of the Eighteenth Amendment to the Constitution. Almost immediately, organized crime stepped in to meet the demand. Booze was distilled in secret labs and smuggled across the border. To be served a drink, you had to go to a clandestine bar (or speakeasy), which could be busted at any time by the Feds. If it was, though, you would not have been arrested. During Prohibition it was not illegal to drink alcoholic beverages or even to possess them   only to manufacture, sell or transport them.

The Eighteenth Amendment was repealed by the Twenty-first Amendment in 1933, but that didn't end Prohibition throughout the United States. Though the federal government was no longer involved, several states maintained their own proscriptions against alcohol, with Mississippi the last to end them in 1966. There remain counties throughout the South that are still "dry."

During prohibition you had to fight for your right to party.

THE PUPIL IS THE BLACK
SPOT IN THE MIDDLE OF THE EYE

The pupil, at the center of the iris, appears to be a black spot. Actually, it's clear, of course. The black we see is the darkness of the inside of the eye.

When flash pictures are taken under dim light conditions, the pupil is wide open. It's the light reflecting off the retina back through the pupil that gives you that red-eyed Terminator look.

THE PYRAMIDS OF EGYPT
WERE BUILT BY SLAVE LABOR

Since outdoor work involving heavy lifting is not our idea of a desirable job, most of us assume that pyramid building required slaves, whipped by overseers and worked to death by the thousands.

Herodotus, the Greek historian, helped establish this misconception, writing that the Great Pyramid was built by over 100,000 slaves.

Actually, local farmers were drafted into service between July and November, when the Nile flooded the fields and farming was impossible, and only about 4,000 were used at a time. Workers were paid; in a sense it was a public works project. According to one of the foremen, they were so pleased to labor for the greater glory of their king that they worked "without a single man getting exhausted, without a man thirsting," and "came home in good spirits, sated with bread, drunk with beer, as if it were the beautiful festival of a god." Bet your boss thinks you feel the same way about working for him.

QUICKSAND SUCKS ITS
VICTIMS UNDER THE SURFACE

If jungle movies have taught us anything, it's that anyone who steps into quicksand is a goner—the ungodly goop sucks its victim inexorably down to a dark and clammy doom. The more the victim struggles, the more rapidly he is pulled under, till at last only a des-

perate hand reaches up, clawing franti-
cally for a moment, only to relax in
death and slip under the surface.

When loose, fine sand becomes so
saturated with water that it acts as a
liquid, you have the substance called
quicksand. It usually develops near the
mouths of rivers, near a shoreline over
a sublayer of clay or above an under-
ground spring that constantly pumps
water up through a body of sand.
Quicksand is more buoyant than
water, and a body will float in it about twice as well. It can be dangerous, as a person who struggles in it will tend to work himself
deeper and deeper. On the other hand, a person who remains
relaxed will not sink much above his armpits. The best way to get
out of quicksand is to slowly "swim" through it, or lay on your back
and then roll out of it.

It isn't called "quicksand" because it will quickly pull you
under, as the word suggests. *Quick* is used in the old sense meaning "alive"—it is "alive sand," just like mercury was called "quick-
silver." The same meaning shows up in the Old West expression,
"There's only two kinds of gunfighters, the quick and the dead."
Though it makes just as much sense if taken to mean "the fast and
the dead," it actually meant "the living and the dead."

QWERTY KEYBOARD DESIGNED FOR EFFICIENCY

Those who type may assume that the odd arrangement of the keys,
called the QWERTY keyboard after the first six letters on the upper
left, is the result of research into human engineering. Surely a
great deal of thought went into this standardized layout, and
lengthy testing proved it the most efficient possible design.

Actually, it is nothing of the sort. Research has indicated that
nearly any other possible arrangement would be easier for the
typist, but the QWERTY system is now so entrenched that various
attempts to replace it have failed.

In the 1870s, when Christopher Latham Sholes invented the
typewriter, he laid the keys out in the most logical fashion—in
alphabetical order. When he tried to type on it, though, he found

that the keys tended to jam when his typewriter was used at any great speed. The problem was that too many frequently used letters were placed close together and tended to interfere with each other. Sholes' brother-in-law, a mathematician, devised the QWERTY layout—by separating the most commonly used letters as far apart on the keyboard as possible. The layout added a slight, built-in delay to the typing process, for the benefit of the typewriter, not the typist.

With a marketing strategy ahead of its time, Sholes took the biggest apparent drawback in his design—the scrambled keyboard—and made it an asset. Bending the truth about 180 degrees, he claimed that the QWERTY layout had been arrived at scientifically and that it represented the fastest possible way to type. (True only if the alternative was spending half your time untangling keys.) A British authority on the history of the typewriter has described Sholes' ruse as "probably one of the biggest confidence tricks of all time."

Long after the last mechanical typewriters have been melted down for manhole covers, we will sit at our twenty-first-century computing consoles and struggle with the keyboard that was laid out to meet nineteenth-century engineering requirements. About the only thing that can be said in its favor is that you can spell out the word *typewriter* using only the letters in the top row.

RATTLESNAKES RATTLE BEFORE THEY STRIKE; THEIR NUMBER OF RATTLES TELLS A SNAKE'S AGE

Many snakes vibrate their tails when threatened; the rattlesnake, equipped with its unique rattle, is able to make this movement audible. Nevertheless, the fact that you can sometimes hear the rattlesnake's warning does not offer much comfort. What we call a warning is just a nervous reaction, and the rattlesnake is perfectly capable of striking without the slightest warning when startled.

A rattle is added to the rattlesnake's tail each time it sheds its skin, inspiring the myth that you can tell a rattlesnake's age by the number of its rattles. In fact, how often a snake sheds its skin depends on how much food it is getting—it may not shed its skin at all in a lean year, but may shed two or three times in a good one. Rattles also wear off from rubbing against hard surfaces. Rattlesnakes in the wild rarely have more than 14 rattles; in captivity they may sport as many as 29.

RAW EGGS ARE HEALTHIER THAN COOKED

Anyone who squirmed during *Rocky* when they saw the hero chugging down a dozen raw eggs must have assumed there was some purpose to it. After all, a guy who dedicated his life to prize-fighting would have to have a pretty good idea of what was good for him, right? Wrong.

The only thing in raw eggs that is missing from eggs that are well cooked is the bacteria that causes salmonella poisoning.

READING IN DIM LIGHT WILL RUIN YOUR EYES

There is a popular belief that straining your eyes will wear them out. Injury might be caused by reading in dim light, reading too much, reading small print, reading under fluorescent light, lack of glasses, wearing glasses with the improper prescription or even watching too much television. It used to be said that the women who made lace by hand inevitably went blind from having to focus on such close, exacting work.

There is no way that any of these activities can harm your vision. You may get headaches, and the muscles that control the movement of the eye may get tired, but you won't do any permanent damage. As a pamphlet put out by the American Academy of Ophthalmology puts it, "Reading in dim light can no more harm the eyes than taking a photograph in dim light can harm the camera."

Many people believe that it is bad to watch television in a completely darkened room; there should always be a lamp on as well. This belief was successfully promulgated by Philadelphia public relations man J. Robert Mendte, who happened to be working for a company that manufactured lamps.

RED SQUARE WAS NAMED BY THE COMMUNISTS

In the center of Moscow is an 800,000-square-foot paved space. Every May Day throughout the Cold War we saw it filled with Soviet troops, tanks and missile carriers, parading before the geriatric Politburo assembled atop Lenin's Tomb. That this locale was known as Red Square seemed only natural, since it was crawling with commies.

The name Red Square predates the Russian Revolution by about 150 years, however. The marketplace took its name from the Old Russian word *krasnaya*, which translates as both "beautiful" and "red."

REPTILES ARE ALWAYS COLD BLOODED

There are certain basic rules that you were always able to count on. For example, we knew that all mammals bore live young. Then we encountered the duck-billed platypus and five species of spiny anteaters, all of whom lay eggs.

Another rule that seemed immutable is that all reptiles are cold blooded. It is one of the defining characteristics of the group. There is an exception to this rule too, though—the leatherback turtle, at up to 1,600 pounds one of the largest living reptiles. Unlike most sea turtles, the leatherback travels in cold waters as well as tropical. One was discovered off the coast of Nova Scotia, in 45°F water, with a body temperature of 77°F. Reptiles normally depend on outside sources for heat, but the leatherback turtle is able to regulate its own body temperature.

Scientist James Spotila of Drexel University has termed the leatherback a *gigantotherm*, theorizing that it maintains body heat largely through its huge size. He speculates that dinosaurs may have been warm blooded in the same sense—most of them were so large that it took a long time for the heat generated by their metabolism to radiate away. According to Spotila's calculations, a 10-ton "cold-blooded" dinosaur could have maintained the same body temperature as today's mammals, even in cold regions.

THE RICKSHAW WAS AN ORIENTAL INVENTION

The rickshaw was not a traditional Oriental conveyance. It was introduced to Japan in 1869 by a Baptist missionary, Jonathan Scobie, who had it built to transport his invalid wife through the crowded streets of Yokohama. It was based on an eighteenth-century French *brouette*, a wheeled version of the sedan chair, and became popular as a sort of muscle-powered taxicab. The name comes from the Japanese for man (*jin*), strength (*riki*) and vehicle (*sha*). Scobie began producing them to provide employment for his converts.

ROBERT KENNEDY SAID, "YOU SEE THINGS AND YOU SAY, 'WHY?' BUT I DREAM OF THINGS THAT NEVER WERE AND ASK 'WHY NOT?'"

When W. P. Kinsella used these words in his 1982 novel *Shoeless Joe*, which inspired the movie *Field of Dreams*, he attributed them to Bobby Kennedy. The words had been associated with Robert Kennedy since he used them as the theme of his 1968 presidential campaign, but they were not his. His brother John had used them in a 1963 speech and correctly attributed them to George Bernard Shaw. They became attached to Bobby as a kind of epitaph after his assassination, symbolic of the idealism many people attributed to him.

THE ROLLS ROYCE IS THE WORLD'S FINEST AUTOMOBILE

When people imagine the luxuries they could buy if they won the lottery, a Rolls Royce is usually somewhere in the picture. Rolls and riches seem to go together. The Queen of England has a few, as did the Beatles and Elvis. Henry Ford owned one, the Bhagwan Shree Rajneesh owned scores and the Shah of Iran had one of every model ever made. Even Brezhnev, Stalin and Lenin had them—the father of Soviet communism actually bought nine, including one with a half-track arrangement for use in snow. If people who can buy whatever they want choose the Rolls Royce, it must be the

world's finest automobile, right?

Talk to an honest Rolls Royce owner before you decide.

Al Goldstein, publisher of *Screw* magazine, used to rail in his editorials against his unreliable Rolls and the poor service he was able to get for it in New York.

Rocky Aoki, the founder of the Benihana restaurant chain and owner of eight Rolls Royces, has described it as "very unreliable car. Very costly to maintain. One time I buy car from Sheik of Bahrain. Engine blew up."

"It's a piece of crap," says Alexander Karas, whose Baltimore limousine service owns six of them. He claims they break down so much "you almost need a mechanic with you in the trunk." Karas points out that the Rolls is retrograde technologically. They've hardly improved their engines since World War II. Never able to build their own transmission, they buy them from American manufacturers. Their air-conditioning system is made by General Motors, and their shocks by a company in France. Their drive train is the same one that Disney uses in the antique cars at the Magic Kingdom.

The old saying about the price of a yacht is that if you have to ask, you can't afford it. That goes for the repair bills on a Rolls Royce as well.

One strange myth that has attached itself to the Rolls is that, when a Rolls breaks down anywhere in the world, the company will promptly dispatch the parts necessary to fix it. Obviously, with the Rolls' undistinguished record for reliability, such a policy would have been ruinous. The company has succeeded in going bankrupt without it.

ROSY CHEEKS MEAN GOOD HEALTH

Ruddy cheeks have long been associated with health and vigor, and pallid ones with illness. Just as often, though, rosy cheeks indicate illness. In children, the cheeks often redden with the onset of a fever. Certain forms of tuberculosis and heart disease also cause that robust-looking high color, as well as heavy drinking.

ROUGH RIDERS WERE LED BY THEODORE ROOSEVELT; RODE UP SAN JUAN HILL

"The Rough Riders" was the nickname given to the First Regiment of U.S. Cavalry Volunteers that Theodore Roosevelt organized for the Spanish-American War, bringing together cowboys, miners, law-enforcement officials and college athletes. They trained for two months as a mounted cavalry regiment in Texas before shipping out to Cuba. Contrary to popular belief, they were not led by Roosevelt but by Colonel Leonard Wood. One of the few events anyone remembers about the Spanish-American War is the Rough Riders' charge up San Juan Hill, routing the Spanish and turning the tide in the conflict. Though we picture the Rough Riders on horseback, their charge was made largely on foot. There was only room on the troop ships for the officers' horses, and the enlisted men's mounts were left behind. Trudging around Cuba, the troops soon renamed themselves "Wood's Weary Walkers."

RUSH LIMBAUGH AND HIS "FORMERLY NICOTINE-STAINED FINGERS"

There have been a number of attempts to catch conservative talk show host Rush Limbaugh in inaccuracies. Many of the errors attributed to him are debatable, but there is one falsehood that he repeats so often over the air that it has become one of his catchphrases. An ex-smoker, Limbaugh often tells his listeners that he is holding something in his "formerly nicotine-stained fingers." This is a blatant untruth. It's not the nicotine that causes stains on the fingers of cigarette smokers, but the tar. Nicotine is colorless.

ST. PATRICK WAS IRISH

St. Patrick is the patron saint of Ireland, but he himself was not a child of the old sod. He was British, and his claim to fame was converting the Irish to Christianity. His mission to Ireland late in the fifth century was his second visit—on the first occasion he had been taken there as a captive of Irish pirates and sold into slavery. St. Patrick never got over that early experience and never felt quite at home in Ireland. He described the inhabitants of the Emerald Isle as "savage barbarians." According to E. J. Dillon, author of a book on St. Patrick, "Even at the end of his life he expected daily a violent death, to be robbed or reduced to slavery."

As an Englishman, he might have felt equally nervous at New York's St. Paddy's Day parade.

SALTPETER IS A SEXUAL DEPRESSANT

The rumor tends to go around in boys' schools, army mess halls and prison dining halls that the food is being doctored with saltpeter. Saltpeter is supposed to possess the power to diminish the male sexual drive, helpful to the authorities in situations where rampant unrelieved horniness could lead to trouble.

The main application of saltpeter, or potassium nitrate, is as an ingredient in gunpowder. It has no effect whatsoever on the sex drive, and to the best of anyone's knowledge has never been used for that purpose. It has certain medicinal properties—it is a mild diuretic and a muscle relaxant—but in heavy doses causes such dangerous side effects that no one but a psychotic would lace food with it.

Granted, that doesn't necessarily exclude boys' school administrators.

SANDWICHES WERE INVENTED BY THE EARL OF SANDWICH

England's John Montagu, the fourth Earl of Sandwich (1718-1792), is often described as the inventor of the meal that bears his name. A prime candidate for Gamblers Anonymous, he was so reluctant to leave the gaming table that he came up with a way to take his meals there. With a piece of meat stuck between two slices of bread, he could hold his cards with one hand and his lunch in the other.

The idea that he *invented* the sandwich is preposterous, though. Peasants in medieval Europe used to bring sandwiches of bread and cheese with them for lunch when they worked in the fields. Arabs had been stuffing pita bread with meat for centuries. And during Passover, the ancient Jews made sandwiches of nuts and fruit between matzoh bread. One of the great things about being part of the nobility is that you get a lot of stuff you're not entitled to, including credit for inventing something everyone already knew about.

It's just as well that the earl became famous for the sandwich rather than for some of his other accomplishments. These included leading the government's prosecution of a former close friend, using his position as first lord of the Admiralty to take more than the acceptable amount of bribes and keeping most of the British fleet in European waters during the American Revolution, contributing to Britain's loss.

By the way, the Sandwich Islands (now the Hawaiian Islands) were named after him, not after the bread-and-meat combo.

SAP FROM TREES MESSES UP CARS PARKED UNDERNEATH

The sticky stuff speckling your car after you've parked under a tree is generally assumed to be sap. In fact, it's "honeydew," a lovely term for bug crap. Tiny aphids, also known as plant lice, process the sap of certain deciduous trees and produce the sweet, sticky digestive product. Honeydew is believed to have been the manna from the Heavens described in the Old Testament. Falling on the ground, it's an important source of nutrition for ants. Falling on your car, it's an important source of income for the car wash.

SARDINES ARE A KIND OF FISH

When you're fishing, the only way you could catch a sardine is if you hook a can of them that's lying on the bottom among the old tires and outboard motors. There's no such fish as a sardine. The name is applied to any small fish that are packaged in sardine cans, usually small herring or pilchard.

The reason sardines are packed so tightly is not from some noble desire to give you your money's worth. The oil they're packed in costs more by volume than the sardines themselves, so the more sardines, the greater the profit.

SCALPING WAS A NATIVE AMERICAN CUSTOM

It's true that American Indians used to scalp their foes; they didn't have a monopoly on the custom, however. English, French,

Spanish and Dutch colonists used scalping as a way to clear their territories of Indian residents, paying frontiersmen a bounty for each scalp turned in. Indians that were allied with settlers got in on the deal when they warred with other tribes. In 1703 the going rate for an Indian scalp in Massachusetts was £12; 20 years later it had gone up to the princely sum of £100. The payoff was a boon to morally challenged types, as it didn't matter whether the scalps were garnered from enemies, allies, women or children. The peaceful Beothuk tribe of Newfoundland was completely wiped out due to scalp bounties paid by the French. During the French and Indian Wars, payments were, for the first time, made for the scalps of enemy whites. When Indian tribes, the Iroquois in particular, began routinely scalping encroaching white settlers, Europeans suddenly awakened to the barbarity of the nasty business and generously credited the Native Americans with its origination. Nevertheless, well into the nineteenth century, bounties were paid on Apache scalps until a public outcry forced an end to it.

SCOTS INVENTED KILTS, GOLF AND BAGPIPES

—Though most people think of the kilt as the native costume of Scotland, Scotsmen didn't start wearing the kilt as we know it until the eighteenth century. Before that they wore knee-length tartan shirts, belted in the middle. Worse yet, the kilt was invented by of all people an Englishman, Thomas Rawlinson, around 1727. In 1745 the British Parliament banned them in an attempt to weaken Scottish national identity at a time of rebellion. Of course, once the English made it clear that the kilts annoyed them, the Scottish knew they had a good thing going. Every high school dress code suffers the same fate.

—Though St. Andrews, the world's most famous golf course, was established in Scotland in 1522, the game did not originate there. The Romans played a version of it with a ball stuffed with feathers—they called it *paganica*, "the country game." It probably came to Britain with the Roman legions. The

Dutch had a game called *kolf* or *kolven*, in which a tally is kept of the number of strokes a player requires to hit a post with his ball. The Flemish had a game called *chole*, which used clubs of a similar design. The Scots can be credited with developing the modern version of the game and organizing the mania.

—The bagpipe also has its origins elsewhere. The first bagpipes were fashioned from reeds stuck in goatskin bags in the Middle East several centuries before the birth of Christ. The instrument spread across the Mediterranean and throughout Europe, and didn't reach Scotland until the early fifteenth century. Before its arrival, the Scottish national instrument had been the harp. The bagpipe found its natural home in Scotland, whose stoic people were already inured to suffering.

SHERLOCK HOLMES SAID, "ELEMENTARY, MY DEAR WATSON" IN SIR ARTHUR CONAN DOYLE'S STORIES

Sherlock Holmes' signature line appears nowhere in the four novels and 56 short stories that Sir Arthur Conan Doyle wrote about the sleuth's adventures. In *The Crooked Man*, Dr. Watson, the narrator, recounts this exchange with Holmes:

"Excellent!" I cried.

"Elementary," said he.

Clive Brook, playing Holmes in the 1929 film *The Return of Sherlock Holmes*, was the first to utter the immortal words "Elementary, my dear Watson."

Sherlock Holmes' trademark deerstalker hat is not mentioned in any of the books either. That was the contribution of William Gillette, who played him onstage.

Though Holmes was supposed to have used a touch of cocaine from time to time, he never said, "Quick, Watson, the needle!" as some have maliciously averred.

SILENCERS CAN MAKE A REVOLVER SILENT

In the movies, after the villain screws a small silencer onto the end of his pistol, the resulting shot is almost silent—what spy novelists describe as a "whisper." It's not that easy—or quiet. First of all, "silencer" is a misleading term—the cognoscenti call it a "suppressor," as it suppresses sound more than silences it. The hope is to dampen the noise enough that it will not carry far or be easily identified as gunfire. It works on the same principle as a car muffler, and real silencers are considerably larger than what you usually see on TV. A .45 caliber pistol requires one nearly the size of a liter-sized soda bottle.

A silencer cannot be effectively employed on a revolver—too much of the explosive force escapes from the gap between the cylinder and the barrel. On a semiautomatic, there is still the considerable racket of the action feeding in a new cartridge. Any round that breaks the sound barrier—a 9 mm, for example, but not the slower .45—will make a sonic crack, silenced or not.

"SILENT CAL" COOLIDGE DIDN'T LIKE TO TALK

A historian has noted that when it comes down to it, most of the presidents will be remembered, at best, in one line—Washington was the father of our country, Lincoln freed the slaves, Ford fell down a lot. If you asked a hundred people to supply that line about Martin Van Buren or James Polk, though, you'd probably draw a blank. One of the few who has retained some sort of image was Calvin Coolidge, President during the Roaring Twenties. He was known as "Silent Cal." One of the jokes about him was that a woman sitting next to him at a dinner party told him she'd bet her husband she could get him to say three words. "You lose," was his reply. Another was that he returned from church one day and his wife asked him what the sermon had been about. "Sin," was his answer. "What did the minister say about sin?" asked his wife. "He was against it," Coolidge answered.

Actually, neither of these stories was true. They were just jokes going around that were hung on Coolidge because they fit his image. That image was created and managed by Coolidge himself. Though Coolidge was cautious in his public utterances—as he observed, "If you don't say anything, you won't be called upon to repeat it"—he gave more interviews to the press than any President before him, and transcripts reveal he could be quite garrulous, though much of what he said was off the record. Some journalists at the time found him so forthcoming they actually dubbed him the "talkative President," though it didn't occur to any of them to inquire whether he wore boxers or briefs.

THE SLAVE TRADE SERVED MOSTLY THE AMERICAN SOUTH

Did most of the Africans that were brought across the Atlantic in bondage end up on selling blocks in the American South? Surprisingly, no. Though the South had a far larger slave population at the time of liberation than any other slave society, the number of slaves brought in was relatively small. *In The Atlantic Slave Trade: A Census*, Philip D. Curtin reveals that the 427,000 slaves imported into the United States represented only 4.5% of the slaves brought to the New World. The other 95.5% went to plantations in the Caribbean Islands and in Latin America, especially Brazil, which received 10 times the number sent to the United States.

It was only in the United States that slave populations grew naturally, so that by 1865 there were 4 million slaves and another half million free African-Americans. In every other slave society in the Western Hemisphere, births did not keep up with deaths, largely due to disease. The French islands of Martinique and Guadeloupe took in 656,000 slaves, but had less than 20% of that number at the time of emancipation.

SNOWFLAKES—NO TWO ARE EXACTLY ALIKE

The six-sided shape of snowflakes had been observed by Johannes Kepler in the seventeenth century, but people weren't aware of their actual structure until quite recently. Wilson Alwyn ("Snowflake") Bentley, of Jericho, Vermont, began photographing snowflakes through a microscope in 1885. In 1931 his photographs were published in a book, *Snow Crystals*. The fact that no two of the thousands of snow crystals shown in the book were identical gave rise to the idea that no two snowflakes are ever alike.

This truism has long been disputed on logical grounds. That "no two snowflakes are exactly alike" cannot possibly be established—all we can say is that there is an astonishing variety of shapes snowflakes can take considering that they are all six sided and all their angles are either 60 or 120 degrees. Nevertheless, the statement could still be credibly uttered until a few years ago, when Nancy Knight, a visiting scientist at the National Center for Atmospheric Research, discovered among snowflake photos she had taken from a research plane two that were *exactly* alike. You'd think such a find would be at least as widely known as Liz Taylor's current marital status, but Ms. Knight's discovery, though included in the *Bulletin of the American Meteorological Society*, was ignored by the *National Enquirer*.

SOCIAL SECURITY RECIPIENTS ARE ONLY GETTING BACK WHAT THEY PUT IN

Social Security enjoys a special place among entitlements because, after all, most of those collecting it have paid into the system all their lives. Social Security presents itself as a pension plan rather than a welfare service, and rich retirees feel that they are as entitled to their monthly checks as are those who rely on it as their sole source of income.

Unfortunately, Social Security never operated as a pension plan, in which contributions would have been invested, but a "pay as you go" plan, in which recipients are paid by current contributors. When the program began, the premiums were small, as there were lots of workers per retiree—47 to one in 1940. Throughout the last three decades, benefits have gone up dramatically, even as the proportion of workers to retirees has dropped, to four to one by 1970. Naturally premiums have gone up, to the point where they take a larger bite out of the average paycheck than income tax, and today's workers are subsidizing the elderly at a level they themselves will never enjoy.

The ideal year in which to retire was 1980, when average retirees received a windfall of $59,875 more in benefits than they had contributed in taxes. Within six years of retiring, they had gotten back every dollar they ever put into the system. On the other hand, average retirees in 2020 are expected to receive $35,000 less than they contributed, if even that. By that time there will be barely two workers for each retiree, and they will have to turn over a third of their salaries to support the system.

There are private pension plans that function this way—they're called pyramid schemes and their operators are prosecuted for fraud.

SOS MEANS "SAVE OUR SHIP"

The international distress signal SOS does not stand for "Save Our Ship" or anything else for that matter. It is simply the easiest, most recognizable signal to send out in Morse code: three dots, three dashes and three dots again.

Now that most radio communication is conducted verbally, rather than in Morse code, the SOS signal is largely obsolete. "Mayday" is the current distress call, and it has a more picturesque background than SOS. It has nothing to do with a day in May, but comes from the French for "help me," or *m'aidez*.

SPANISH FLY IS AN APHRODISIAC

The aphrodisiacal properties of Spanish fly have been a staple of locker-room banter for generations. Administered in the proper dosages, it is supposed to turn a man into a pile-driver of pulsating potency, and a woman into the slave of insatiable sexual desire (the latter sometimes described as a young man's dream and an older man's nightmare).

Though medical research presses ahead, there is as yet no such thing as an aphrodisiac. Spanish fly, whose reputation goes back centuries, would seem to be an odd candidate. It is made from the crushed shells of blister beetles, and its active ingredient is *cantharidin*. It causes diarrhea, vomiting, depression, internal bleeding, urinary pain and in sufficient doses, death.

How this came to be considered an aphrodisiac can only be understood through the principles of medieval magic, in this case the Law of Similarity. This holds that if lust gives you a burning sensation in your loins, and if Spanish Fly gives you an extreme burning sensation in your loins, then Spanish Fly must provoke extreme lust. This may not seem too convincing, but people weren't as logical in those days. Not like today, when we'll buy a particular brand of jeans because the model in the ad looks sexy in them.

SPEAKERS STAND BEHIND A PODIUM

The piece of furniture politicians stand behind when they give a speech, and on which they bang their fists when they mention their vile opponents, is generally referred to as a "podium." We should be so lucky—if they stood behind the podium we might not see them. The podium is the raised platform or stage on which a speaker stands. The boxy thing they stand behind is called a lectern.

THE SPEED OF SOUND IS A CONSTANT

The speed of light is one of the constants of the universe, and many assume that the speed of sound is one as well. Certainly, fighter pilots routinely throw around Mach numbers (the ratio of the speed of an object to the speed of sound in the surrounding medium) as though the speed of sound were a constant. The figure 760 mph is what they have in mind, but that's based on sound's speed through air at sea level and at 0°C. At 40,000 feet, the speed of sound is 660 mph. In a vacuum there is obviously no speed of sound at all.

The speed of sound is considerably different in other mediums as well. Sound travels faster through solids than through liquids, and faster through liquids than through gases. It travels at 3,300 mph in water, 11,000 mph in steel and 13,000 mph in glass.

Water is a far better transmitter of sound than air. In 1960 Columbia University scientists detonated depth charges off the coast of Australia. Two hours and 24 minutes later, the sound reached a listening post in Bermuda, halfway around the globe. Oklahoma County Jail prisoners have discovered water's excellent property as a sound transmitter. It is reported that they communicate with each other by shouting into the toilet bowls.

Another "constant" that is subject to change is the boiling point of water, often given as 212°F, or 100°C. This temperature is only true at sea level—water requires a lower temperature to boil at higher altitudes, and boils at room temperature in a vacuum.

SPERM WHALES NAMED
BECAUSE OF THEIR SPERM

The sperm whale is one of those creatures that helps keep things lively for boys in the third grade, along with the "robin red breast" and "titmouse." To bring the excitement to a fever pitch, you should know that that other classroom favorite, Moby Dick, was, in fact, a sperm whale.

Sperm whales don't have any special association with sperm. When they were caught and cut open by early whalers, their snouts yielded gobs of a waxy substance that looked a lot like you-know-what. Being probably not much higher evolved on the innuendo scale than the average third-grader, the sailors named it *spermacetti*, the "seed of the whale." In fact, spermacetti has nothing to do with reproduction, but is part of a whale's sonar system and may help protect the whale against deep sea pressures.

Napoleon contemplating the Sphinx.

THE SPHINX'S NOSE WAS
SHOT OFF BY NAPOLEON'S TROOPS

Legend has it that the Great Sphinx at Giza lost its 4,400-year-old nose to Napoleonic troops who occupied Egypt. Some say the ignorant Frenchmen used it for target practice; others say that Napoleon, convinced that its smile mocked him, ordered his gunners to wipe it off its face.

Actually, the nose was broken off 500 years earlier by Saim-el-Dahr, an Islamic militant who considered the pagan idol blasphemous.

SPRINGSTEEN'S "BORN IN THE
U.S.A." WAS A PATRIOTIC ANTHEM

When Bruce Springsteen's "Born in the U.S.A." came out in June 1984, it was regarded as the anthem of a renewed American pride. It hit the country at the time that Ronald Reagan was at the peak of his popularity, and Rambomania ran rampant. Sometimes it seemed that all three represented different facets of the same *zeitgeist*. Crowds at Springsteen concerts waved flags and stadium banners that read: "Bruce—The Rambo of Rock." Larry Berger, program director of New York's WPLJ-FM, said of Springsteen, "He's a spokesman for patriotism. He's the Ronald Reagan of rock 'n' roll." Reagan himself got into the act; in a campaign appearance in New Jersey, he paid homage to the state's native son: "America's future rests in a thousand dreams. It rests in the message of hope in the songs of a man so many Americans admire, Bruce Springsteen."

To Springsteen, who had written "Born in the U.S.A." as a

Vietnam veteran's bleak lament about betrayal and abandonment, all this was rather perplexing. Onstage, he rhetorically wondered which of his albums President Reagan had listened to. (A Reagan aide claimed that Reagan enjoyed listening to all of the Boss' music, and if you can picture that, you have a lively imagination.)

"'Born in the U.S.A.' has been fabulously misheard and misread," observed rock critic Greil Marcus. "Clearly the key to the enormous explosion of Bruce's popularity is the misunderstanding of that song. He is a tribute to the fact that people hear what they want."

SQUIRRELS PUT AWAY NUTS FOR THE WINTER

It seems commendable that squirrels would prepare for winter by stashing away a plentiful supply of nuts and seeds to see them through. Their foresight does not seem so impressive when you discover that the squirrels don't actually remember where they bury the stuff for longer than about 20 minutes. Fortunately they have a good sense of smell and, after sniffing around, dig up whatever hoard they can locate, usually one put away by some other squirrel. Squirrels are estimated to find only about a tenth of the nuts they stash, a poor return on their investment.

THE STAR OF DAVID WAS
AN ANCIENT SYMBOL OF JUDAISM

How long has the six-pointed Star of David been the symbol of Judaism? Judaism is approaching its sixth millennium, but the *mogen David* was not associated with the religion until the seventeenth century, when it was adopted as an official symbol by Jewish communities in Europe. Since then it has appeared on synagogues, Jewish tombstones, early Zionist literature and the flag of Israel. Before that it was used since ancient times as a magical symbol or decoration of no particular religious significance. It was even carved into medieval cathedrals.

STARS—ON A CLEAR NIGHT
YOU CAN SEE A MILLION OF THEM

The number of stars we can see in the sky is often used as a synonym for infinity, like the number of grains of sand on a beach. Even on a clear, moonless night away from city lights, though, you can't count more than about 4,000 individual stars with the naked eye.

Of course, that's not to say they're not there. Seven-power binoculars bring about 50,000 into view, and the telescope at California's Palomar Observatory has enabled scientists to photograph more than a billion.

It is impossible to determine the actual number of stars in the universe. Even if we get above our own atmosphere, which blots out most of them, "empty" space still contains enough floating dust (one particle per 100,000 cubic meters) to obscure our view of distant stars. It is estimated that space dust falls to the surface of Earth at the rate of one particle per square centimeter per day.

STEAM IS THE CLOUDY MIST THAT COMES OUT OF A TEAPOT

Most people think of steam as the white, cloudy vapor that comes out of a steam locomotive or teakettle, but it is not. Real steam, the gaseous form of water, is invisible. What you are able to see are the tiny drops of water that condense as the steam cools off. The small clear space between the tea kettle and the visible mist is, in fact, steam.

Those bubbles coming up through boiling water also contain steam.

STEP ON A RUSTY NAIL AND YOU'LL GET TETANUS

Tetanus, otherwise known as lockjaw, is caused by the toxin produced by the bacterium called *Clostridium tetani*. You'll want to avoid the little bugger at all costs—one milligram of its toxin is enough to kill about 20 million people. It's found in the feces of infected animals, especially domestic and farm animals. The disease can enter the body through any open wound or animal bite; it does not require a deep puncture wound such as stepping on a rusty nail produces. Fortunately, there's an effective vaccine.

A pocked and pitted rusty nail might provide an efficient delivery vehicle by which the toxin might get into your bloodstream, but there is nothing special about the nail itself. It could be perfectly sterile.

THE STOMACH IS THE MAIN ORGAN OF DIGESTION

Most people think of the stomach as the main organ of digestion, but not much more food gets digested in the stomach than in the mouth. Digestion, the process of converting food into use by the body, takes place mainly in the small intestine, which is about 22 feet long in humans. The stomach serves mainly to store the food we eat and to break it down with digestive fluids—hydrochloric acid and enzymes—into chyme, a semifluid form that can be absorbed by the small intestine.

A person can live after his or her stomach has been removed completely.

SUCKING VENOM OUT OF A SNAKEBITE HELPS A VICTIM SURVIVE

If you got bitten by a poisonous snake, it used to be believed that your best chance of survival lay in getting someone to suck out the venom. Your survival might be determined by how good a friend you had handy, depending on where you had been bitten. Older first-aid manuals even recommend slashing the skin around the bite mark in order to bleed out more of the venom.

Thinking has changed. Blood travels so fast through the body that any slashing or sucking of the wound is considered unlikely to stop the flow of the snake venom and is liable to increase the dangers of shock and infection. When someone is bitten by a snake, the latest advice is to wash and disinfect the wound, have the victim lie down and get medical attention as soon as possible. Don't put on a tourniquet either—you're only likely to damage more tissue. It's also recommended that you kill the snake and take it along so its venom can be identified, and to let it know how annoyed you are.

SUICIDE IS MOST COMMON DURING THE HOLIDAYS

Many of us react negatively to the consumerism and forced gaiety of the holiday season, and can easily imagine how hard it is for those whose lives are nothing to Ho, Ho, Ho about. The arrival of another fruitcake might be enough to push some people over the edge. TV helps support the belief—it can be counted on to mention the suicide rate as a counterpoint to the holiday stories, just as it never lets Thanksgiving pass without a broadcast from a soup kitchen. Why let the facts get in the way of a sobering irony?

Suicides are actually less common in December and January than at any other time of the year. Fewer suicides are committed on holidays in general than at other times. The National Center for Health Statistics identifies April as the month when rates peak; it may just be a coincidence that death and taxes seem to go together.

Summer and early fall also experience a high incidence rate.

If not suicide, what about the holiday blues, or (to give it its clinical designation) Christmas Depression Syndrome? Actually, psychiatric admissions also tend to be lower during December.

Where does this belief in high levels of holiday suicides come from, besides some people's need for morbid irony? There is evidence that it may have been floated by the folks at the suicide prevention hotlines. Charitable donations are highest during the season of giving, and they want to make sure they're remembered too. If that doesn't satisfy your appetite for morbid irony, nothing will.

SUMO WRESTLERS CAN WITHDRAW THEIR TESTICLES

In *You Only Live Twice*, James Bond witnesses Japanese commandos enthusiastically booting each other in the groin without apparent discomfort. This strikes him as a pretty useful talent for a guy in his line of work—he never knows when he might require such a defense against agents of SMERSH, or cocktail waitresses who don't appreciate his approach. Tiger Tanaka, head of the spy school, explains to Bond that it's an old sumo trick—sumos are able to retract their vulnerable testicles up into the inguinal canal through which they originally descended, "by assiduously massaging those parts" shortly after puberty. It would seem that many have tried this training technique without achieving that outcome.

Actually, shrews, moles and hedgehogs are able to do this, but no humans that we know about. Any man who's gone swimming off the coast of northern California has come close, but not quite.

THE SUN IS CLOSEST TO THE EARTH DURING SUMMER

Strangely enough, the sun is not closer to the earth during summer, nor even the same distance, but farther. On January 1st the sun is approximately 3 million miles closer to the earth than it is on June 1st. (We're referring to winter in the Northern Hemisphere, of course.)

It is the tilt of the earth's axis, not the distance of the earth from the sun, that determines the seasons. The part of the earth receiving the most direct rays from the sun enjoys the most warmth.

THE SUN STANDS STILL AS THE EARTH REVOLVES AROUND IT

The sun is not standing still as the earth revolves around it. To start with, the sun revolves on its own axis, about one turn per 27 days. Then, along with our little solar system, the sun itself is hurtling through space, revolving around the hub of the Milky Way Galaxy at nearly 500,000 miles per hour. The Milky Way isn't staying put either. It's moving at about 1,296,000 miles per hour around the core of the cluster of galaxies of which it is only a small part. At the same time, our cluster of galaxies is moving at enormous speed away from other galaxy clusters. Of course, according to Einstein's theory of relativity, it is impossible to measure absolute motion in space because there is no object in the universe that is absolutely at rest, against which its motion can be measured.

Kind of makes you feel dizzy and insignificant just thinking about it.

SWALLOWS RETURN TO CAPISTRANO EVERY YEAR ON THE SAME DAY

We've seen the movie, heard the song, we know it's true. On precisely March 19 of every year, the swallows faithfully return to the mission of San Juan Capistrano from their winter homes 6,000 miles away in Argentina. How the swallows manage this, what with leap years and all, elevates the feat to something of a miracle. As surely as the swallows flock to the site on the same day every year, so do some 10,000 tourists to see them do it.

The problem is, they don't. Swallows may return to southern California anytime from late February to the end of March. They don't all arrive in a single flock. Not many swallows would even nest around the mission anymore, if it were left up to them. When it was built, it provided a singularly suitable habitat for these cliff dwellers; now it's just one of a number of tall buildings in which they can make their nests. The mission, respectful of the tourist dollar, follows that hallowed religious maxim that "God helps those who help themselves" (a quote that does not appear in the Bible, by the way). It prepares an annual welcoming buffet of tasty bugs to attract the birds.

Many of the tourists who think they are seeing the swallows are actually seeing the common white-throated swift, which stays in California year-round. It's one of those celebrity impersonators.

THE SWASTIKA ORIGINATED AS A NAZI EMBLEM

Somewhere way down on the list of Nazism's crimes is the fact that it forever ruined the swastika as a symbol of anything but evil. The swastika is so closely tied to the Nazis that many people assume it was their creation. In fact, the "broken cross" preceded Hitler by 5,000 years or so and was used by cultures all over the world as a symbol of prosperity and good fortune. It appeared on Mesopotamian coins and in early Christian and Byzantine art, where it was known as the gammadian cross. It also shows up in Scandinavian, Celtic, Chinese, Egyptian and Greek artifacts. It occurs in the carvings of the Central and South American Mayans. It was a common element in Navajo weavings. In fact, the 45th Infantry Division, a National Guard outfit from New Mexico, used a gold swastika on a red background as its emblem. It hastily switched to a thunderbird motif at the outset of World War II, and Navajo artists patriotically foreswore further use of their ancient symbol.

The design is most closely identified with the Hindus, who use it to mark the opening pages of account books, thresholds, doors and religious offerings. The word itself comes from the Sanskrit *svastika,* which means, ironically, "conducive to well-being." The Hindus gave a different meaning to the swastika depending on its direction. When the swastika's arms point in a clockwise direction, it is a solar symbol; the counterclockwise swastika symbolizes night, the occult and the goddess of destruction, Kali. The latter would seem the appropriate choice for the Nazis, but they chose to go with the former as their emblem in 1920.

SWEAT CLEANS YOUR SYSTEM

A long night of binge partying may leave you craving a session in the sauna to sweat out the unholy assortment of impurities you busily crammed into your system. Though the sauna may feel good, it can't accomplish that objective. You cannot excrete toxins through the pores of your skin; there is no connection between the organs that clean your system and the perspiration glands. There are two purposes of sweat: heat dissipation and, on the palms of the hands and soles of the feet, to keep those friction surfaces moist.

In his 1960 campaign debates against Kennedy, Nixon's profuse sweating made such a poor impression on the TV audience that it may have cost him the election. That helped keep the system clean, at least for a while.

SWIMMING AFTER EATING POSES A DANGER OF CRAMPS

This staple of parental wisdom was originally propounded by the venerable Red Cross. Those who swam within an hour and a half of eating were supposed to be in danger of getting stomach cramps that would cause them to seize up and drown. In the 1956 edition of its *Life Saving & Water Safety* manual, the organization began to soft-pedal the perils of stomach cramps, but still argued that swimming after eating might "cause the heart to labor unduly," and suggests that that might account for numerous drownings, while at the same time acknowledging that "no definite proof can be elicited for the statement."

The Red Cross no longer has any objection to anyone participating in aquatic activities immediately upon completing a meal, and admits to know ing of no one who has ever drowned as a result of doing so. Some discretion is still advised. After all, if you've just gobbled up a few bacon cheeseburgers, your heart stands a good chance of stopping at any moment, in the water or out.

TARANTULAS ARE POISONOUS SPIDERS

A scene in *Dr. No* has James Bond waking up in bed with a surprise guest. For once it wasn't a blonde, but a big black hairy tarantula placed there by Dr. No's henchman. It crawls up Bond's body as he lies frozen in terror, sweating bullets. At last, after it drops onto the bedding, he smashes it and staggers, nauseated, into the bathroom.

This is the same James Bond who can discourse on topics as varied as jazz, the gold market and the proper temperature to serve sake—and he doesn't know that a tarantula is harmless? The bite of the formidable-looking creature is no more serious than a bee sting. In fact, tarantulas cannot bite at all, as they have no teeth. They can only deliver a sort of pinch with the two clawlike legs that they use to catch and hold insects. Instead of poison, they deliver a catabolic enzyme that turns the captive bug's innards to soup, which tarantulas then suck out.

Armed with this information, you will surely retain your composure if you too should wake up to find one of the furry arachnids sharing your bed.

TARZAN SAID, "ME TARZAN, YOU JANE"

There are two things that we all remember from the soundtracks of the classic Tarzan films. The first is Johnny Weissmuller's inimitable yell. The second is that priceless pickup line, "Me Tarzan, you Jane."

You may not be too surprised to learn that Weissmuller could never actually deliver that yell—it was synthesized from a smorgasbord of sound effects. Technicians blended his own yell with a high C hit by a soprano and a hyena's howl and played the whole thing backward. What you may find harder to believe is that Weissmuller never uttered those unforgettable words. Weissmuller himself,

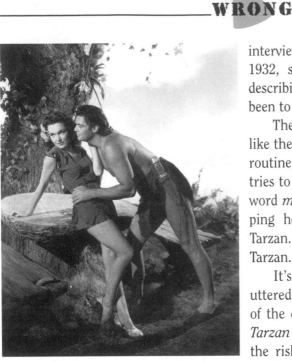

interviewed when the movie was released in 1932, seemed to think he had, modestly describing the extent of his acting as having been to utter, "Me Tarzan, you Jane."

The actual dialogue in the movie is more like the Abbott and Costello "who's on first" routine, a comedy of confusion as Tarzan tries to understand what Jane means by the word *me*. He finally gets it, alternately tapping her and himself as he says: "Jane. Tarzan. Jane. Tarzan. Jane. Tarzan. Jane. Tarzan. Jane. Tarzan. Jane...."

It's possible that Tarzan may have uttered the famous pronouncement in one of the cheesy remakes, such as Bo Derek's *Tarzan the Ape Man*. It doesn't seem worth the risk to find out, though—it has been established that a single close viewing of that particular film can lower your IQ by as much as 15 points.

TEARS FLOW FROM YOUR EYES ONLY

Done with aplomb, weeping can be glamorous. But why does your nose have to run at the same time, spoiling the effect? Surprisingly enough, there's a direct connection. As the tears start to gush, not all the fluid runs down your cheeks. Some of it drains through the *puncta lacrimalia*, a tiny "drain" at the inside corner of your eye, through the *nasolacrimal duct* into your nose. That's where it gets messy.

THE TELEPHONE WAS INVENTED BY ALEXANDER GRAHAM BELL

Like Edison's invention of the lightbulb, Bell's invention of the telephone is less a case of invention than of adding a small incremental improvement to existing technology and then foreseeing its commercial potential. Germans would argue that it was their countryman, Frankfurt physicist John Philip Reis, who was the true father of the telephone. In 1861, 15 years before Bell received his patent, Reis built a crude apparatus that converted the human voice to electrical impulses and transmitted it by wire—he even called it a telephone. It used improvised elements such as a beer barrel cork for a mouthpiece and a sausage skin for a diaphragm, and its sound quality was so poor that MCI would have had a field day running ads against it. There is an argument as to whether it was capable of transmitting intelligible words at all. Reis didn't realize the potential of his device, using it only as a demonstration tool when lecturing on the nature of sound. Nevertheless, Bell was aware of Reis' work, and as late as 1900 the U.S. government continued to harass Bell, claiming he'd concealed his knowledge of Reis' sausage-skin speakers from the patent officers.

Developing the telephone at the same time as Bell was Elisha Gray. Gray was a pioneer in the development of the telegraph and, along with a partner, founded the Western Electric Company. He filed a patent application for his version of the telephone on February 14, 1876, the same day as Bell filed for his, but two hours later. Neither Gray nor Bell had a working telephone at the time—they each filed for improvements they felt would make telephone communication feasible. Both applications were frozen for 90 days so that patent officers could weigh their relative merits. Bell hurried down to the patent office in Washington, D.C., to plead his case, and while there got a look at Gray's application. In order to transmit intelligible speech, Gray's design moved a rod suspended in acidified water to convert sounds into undulating currents. Bell's moved an iron strip through an electromagnetic field for the same purpose, though a handwritten note in the margin of his application referred to the possibility of an acid system. Was this note added after Bell saw Gray's design? No one knows, but Bell's first working telephone used the acid system rather than the one he focused on in his application. It was that acid, spilling on Bell's clothes, that provoked his famous first telephone message, "Mr. Watson, come here, I want you."

Bell received what proved to be the most valuable patent in history, but Gray disputed his claim for years. The Supreme Court, in a divided decision, finally granted the patent to Bell. Since then, the Bell Telephone Company has waged a vigorous campaign promoting its man and denigrating Elisha Gray, whom it has largely consigned to oblivion.

"TELL IT TO THE MARINES!"

The Marine Corps takes a distinct pride in its scrappy reputation. Its motto is "First to Fight," and marines wear T-shirts with messages like: "The U.S. Marines—When It Absolutely, Positively, Has to Be Destroyed Overnight!"

The expression "Tell it to the marines!" seems like yet another of these truculent taunts, suggesting that you might get away with telling it (whatever "it" might be) to someone else, but not to the marines. Actually, the saying did not start out as a boast, but rather as an insult, suggesting that marines were uncommonly gullible. The original version, from Sir Walter Scott, says, "Tell that to the marines—the sailors won't believe it."

TESTOSTERONE MAKES MEN AGGRESSIVE

In our sensitized culture, testosterone is regarded as pretty nasty stuff—it's the hormone of male aggression, fueling everything from Desert Storm to pro football, from biker gangs to heavy metal music. It courses through the veins of every guy with a pickup truck with oversize tires, a rebel flag and a bumper sticker that reads "I'm Only Driving This Way to Piss You Off." G. Gordon Liddy, Sylvester Stallone, Rep. Bob Dornan and Mike Tyson are OD'ing on it.

Recent research suggests that testosterone may be due a reprieve. At the 1995 meeting of the Endocrine Society, researchers reported that it is a *deficiency*, rather than an excess, of testosterone that leads to the sort of bullying behavior associated with the hormone. Fifty-six men who had low testosterone levels were studied, and rather than acting in a passive or timid manner, they tended to be edgy, angry, and irritable. After being given doses of testosterone to bring their levels up to a normal level, the men felt more pleasant and genial.

Granted this is exactly the sort of "startling scientific finding" that is likely to be overturned with the next round of research grants, but it reminds us how risky it is to draw simplistic conclusions about biological destiny. Although men have far greater amounts of testosterone in their blood than women do, it is not correct to describe testosterone as the "male" hormone or estrogen as the "female" hormone. Both sexes require both hormones, and the effects of the hormones are complex and far from fully understood. The brain contains the enzyme *aromatase*, which converts testosterone to estrogen, and it is this hormone that acts on the nerve cells of the brain. Contrary to our cultural clichés, studies conducted on mice by researchers at Rockefeller Institute and at the National Institutes of Health have even suggested that it may be *estrogen* that triggers aggression. It has also been found that excessive drinking can lead to high levels of estrogen production in men.

So next time you venture into a roadside bar, look out for those big-armed, shaggy-bearded, grease-stained, Budweiser-swilling bikers—they may be a bit estrogen crazed.

THANKSGIVING HAS BEEN CELEBRATED EVERY NOVEMBER SINCE PILGRIM DAYS

Schoolchildren are taught that we celebrate Thanksgiving to continue a tradition the Pilgrims established, and they might assume that Thanksgiving has been an unbroken annual tradition since those times.

The Pilgrims did have a three-day feast of thanksgiving sometime in the autumn of 1621. It did not include pumpkin pie, as they had used up their flour supply and couldn't make pie shells—boiled pumpkin was served instead. There is no record that they ate turkey either, though a contemporary letter mentions that they had "fowl" and "deer." The Pilgrims celebrated another day of thanksgiving in 1623, this time in July. Occasional days of thanksgiving were subsequently proclaimed in the colonies for various reasons and on various dates. In 1777 the Continental Congress scheduled one for December 18 to celebrate the defeat of General Burgoyne at Saratoga. In 1789, George Washington proclaimed November 26 a national day of thanksgiving to celebrate the new Constitution. As an annual event the idea didn't catch on, as many of the early presidents, Thomas Jefferson in particular, considered it an inappropriate mingling of church and state.

Thanksgiving as we know it was the result of a campaign by Sarah Josepha Hale, editor of one of the first women's magazines, *Godey's Lady's Book*. After 36 years of promoting the idea, she got Abraham Lincoln to establish it as a national holiday in 1863, to be celebrated ever after on the last Thursday in November. This continued until 1939 when Franklin Roosevelt, in a bid to help shopkeepers extend the Christmas buying season, made it the *third* Thursday of November. Two years later Congress overruled him and put the holiday back where it belonged. For this we should be thankful—one less week of "The Little Drummer Boy" warbling out from the Muzak system.

A THOROUGHBRED
IS ANY HORSE WITH A PEDIGREE, ETC.

The designation *Thoroughbred* does not refer to any horse with a pedigree—it is actually a particular breed of horse, like the Appaloosa, Arabian and Clydesdale.

The Thoroughbred line is less than 350 years old, when King Charles II ordered that James D'Arcy, master of the Royal Stud, deliver to him "12 extraordinarily good colts" per year for the purpose of racing. All modern Thoroughbreds can be traced to three Arabian stallions that were selected to sire the line.

There is also some confusion around the quarter horse. It is not called that because of its size or gait. Nor is it a side of meat you can order from a French butcher. Originally, quarter horses were any horses that were good at running the quarter mile, the standard length of a race at the time the term was coined. Since then, the quarter horse has developed into a distinct breed.

For those whose acquaintance with horses is limited to the coin-operated ones in front of the supermarket, it should be mentioned that a pony is not a baby horse. The term covers a number of breeds of small horse, not measuring over 58 inches tall at the withers. At the same time, a horse can be less than 58 inches tall and still be a horse.

"THOU SHALL NOT KILL"
IS ONE OF THE TEN
COMMANDMENTS

If God really meant this, why didn't he prescribe a vegetarian diet for his chosen people? And why were several of the most righteous heroes of the Old Testament, such as Samson and David, rather accomplished killers? Should we, like some devout Hindus, sweep the path ahead of us as we walk so we don't unwittingly step on a few insects? As it happens, the sixth commandment as we usually hear it has been mistranslated from the Old Hebrew; the proper translation should be "Thou shall not do murder." The Bible assumes that killing is justified in some cases, as when butchering food and in self-defense.

There is a similar confusion between the terms *murder* and *homicide*. They are not synonymous. They both refer to the killing of a person, but a murder is a crime, while a homicide may not be. Homicide is a legally neutral term that can refer to a legally justified killing, as in the still-unsolved death of disco.

THUMBS DOWN WAS THE SIGNAL FOR DEATH IN THE COLISEUM

Every movie about gladiatorial combat in ancient Rome features a scene in which a victorious gladiator, with his sword at the throat of his vanquished foe, turns to the emperor for the verdict. Has his foe earned the right to live to fight another day, or does he deserve the *coup de grace*? If the background music gets ominous, you know what's coming—the thumbs down.

Although such dramas did occur at the Roman Coliseum, historians tell us that "thumbs down" was not the signal for death. The Roman poet and satirist Juvenal wrote that "those who wished the death of the conquered gladiator turned their thumbs toward their breasts, as a signal to his opponents to stab him; those who wished him

"Pollice Verso," 1874, Jean-Léon Gérôme

to be spared, turned their thumbs downwards, as a signal for dropping the sword." Others suggest that the reprieve was signaled by a thumb gesturing away from the body, in a hitchhiking gesture. Body language analyst Desmond Morris says that mercy for the fallen warrior was signified by covering the thumb. Whatever the signals might have been, everyone agrees that thumbs down was not the signal for death.

The confusion arose from a famous 1874 painting by Jean-Léon Gérôme called "Pollice Verso," showing the crowd at the Coliseum all turning their thumbs down to pass judgment on a fallen gladiator. Gérôme's painting was reproduced as an engraving and sold widely. Illustrators copied Gérôme's dramatic image, and it has been permanently fixed in our minds from the movies. Ironically, the title of his painting translates as thumbs *turned*, not thumbs down.

TOILETS ARE A FAIRLY MODERN INVENTION; WERE INVENTED BY THOMAS CRAPPER

The flush toilet did not come into widespread use in Europe and the United States until the late nineteenth century. Previously most city folks used chamber pots, the contents of which they tossed out of windows into the street. It was considered polite to issue a warning cry of "Gardy-loo" (*gardez l'eau*—"look out for the water"), which is supposed to have inspired the British euphemism "the loo" for the toilet.

Sanitation in the middle ages from an old woodcut.

Nevertheless, the flush toilet is not a modern invention, but an ancient one that had lain dormant for over a thousand years awaiting the reintroduction of one vital element—plentiful running water. Until two centuries ago, water had to be carried into most European cities by water carriers. It was only with the installation of water mains and sewer systems that the flush toilet once again became feasible.

Rome in the fourth century provided more water per person than did London for most of the twentieth century, and houses have been unearthed in Pompeii with more than 30 plumbing outlets. Rome in A.D. 315 had 144 water-flushed public latrines. The archaeologist Sir Arthur Evans, excavating the Palace of Knossos in Minoan Crete, found a marble flush toilet that probably once mounted a wooden seat, dating from 2000 B.C. In Mesopotamia there are toilets dating from 1500 B.C. that are still in working order, though you probably have to jiggle the handle a little.

The belief that the modern flush toilet was invented, remarkably enough, by a man named Thomas Crapper is testimony to the staying power of a good hoax. There may have actually been a Thomas Crapper, but his contribution to indoor plumbing was not significant enough to rate a mention outside of Wallace Reyburn's *Flushed with Pride: The Story of Thomas Crapper*, published in England in 1969. The tale includes numerous illustrative anecdotes of questionable veracity, for example, this on the problem of cesspools:

"There was the case of one titled host, at the front door of his country mansion to greet the arrival of a coach full of weekend guests, being called upon to watch in horror as the driveway subsided and they were engulfed in an overflowing cesspool. And, sad to relate, it was not without loss of life."

Crapper's story is told in such a straight-faced manner that many readers took it at face value. Another one of Reyburn's satirical biographies is responsible for the belief that the brassiere was invented by the suspiciously named Otto Titzling.

A Victorian-era toilet.

TO LOSE WEIGHT YOU HAVE TO SHRINK YOUR STOMACH—EATING TOO MUCH STRETCHES IT

Makes sense, doesn't it? By eating too much you've increased the capacity of your stomach so that it now requires more food to feel full. Only by dieting can you shrink that organ to a size where it will feel full with less.

Any doctor will tell you that this is not the case. Eating less may decrease the exterior measurements of your stomach, but the organ itself will not change size. People sometimes have their stomachs stapled so they can eat only small amounts, but you can't achieve the same effect through dieting.

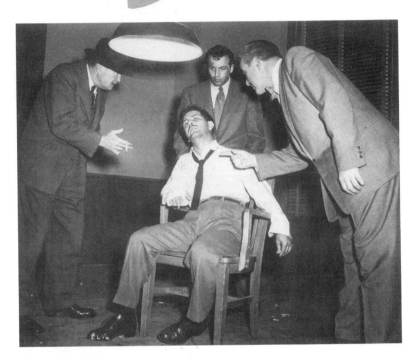

TRUTH SERUM
CAN FORCE YOU TO TELL THE TRUTH

Truth serum, like the lie detector, doesn't live up to its billing.
There is no drug that can force anyone to tell the truth.

The name "truth serum" was first applied to the anesthetic scopolamine by anesthesiologist T. S. House in the early 1920s. He
claimed that when patients were coming out from under the drug,
they could be induced to tell the truth whether they wanted to or
not. The legend of the magical truth serum took hold after a sen-
sational Alabama murder trial, in which a gang of men confessed
to an ax killing after they were administered scopolamine. Since
then, it has figured prominently in detective and spy thrillers,
where it makes a handy plot device.

In fact, neither scopolamine nor any of its successors, sodium amy-
tal and sodium pentothal, can make anyone speak the truth.
Though they may lower inhibitions, a Yale University study concluded that "suspects who would not ordinarily confess under skill-
ful interrogation without drugs are just as likely to continue the
deception while under the influence of drugs."

That old standby alcohol works as well as any so-called truth
serum. Verily, *in vino veritas*—"in wine lies truth."

TURNING ON A LIGHTBULB USES A SURGE OF ELECTRICITY

Those who rationalize their laziness have been known to make a case for not turning off the light when they leave a room. They claim that there's no real savings in turning it off if they'll only turn it on again in a few minutes, as it requires a surge of energy to reheat the filament.

This reasoning is valid in other situations. For example, you clearly save energy by rolling through a stop sign rather than coming to a complete halt, as you may explain to the traffic cop who pulls you over. Lightbulbs are a different matter. The resistance of the filament is so low that heating it requires an inconsequential electrical surge, one that does not translate to any additional cost. When you flick the switch on a 100-watt bulb, your electric meter just starts ringing up that 1.3 cents per hour, more or less. It does add up, as Dad always said.

TURN OF THE CENTURY WILL BE ON JANUARY 1, 2000

Planning a really big party to celebrate the beginning of the twenty-first century on New Year's Eve, 1999? Better lay in lots of beer and Cheetos, because the twenty-first century, the dawn of the third millennium, will not commence until January 1, 2001. Our calendar began with the year 1 (there was no year zero), so the first century did not end until December 31, 100, and the second century did not begin until January 1, 101. And so on. Granted, all this is academic. It's seeing that numeral 2 followed by all those zeros that's going to get everyone excited.

It's understandable that we want to take note of the millennium. Like when your odometer turns over 100,000 miles, it's not something you see every day. At the same time, it's silly to attach cosmic significance to it. It's just a number, rather haphazardly arrived at (See "B.C. and A.D. Mark the Birth of Christ"). By the Chinese reckoning, our year 2000 will be their year 4637, in the Hebrew calendar it will be 5760 and in the Muslim calendar, 1421.

URANUS IS PRONOUNCED "YOUR ANUS"

There are some words that are always good for a laugh—*weenie* and *kumquat* come to mind. The planet Uranus has been a crowd pleaser for years, figuring in any number of sophomoric puns, especially in conjunction with its moons. However, the humorous potential of the seventh planet is based on a mispronunciation of its name. It is the first, rather than the second, syllable that should be stressed. The preferred pronunciation is "YOOR-en-es."

URBAN POLLUTION IS WORSE NOW THAN EVER

When urbanites hear the daily air quality index on the news, they may wistfully hearken back to the age of environmental purity before the widespread use of the automobile. They might be surprised to learn that pollution in the cities of the nineteenth century was worse than it is today.

New York had some 150,000 horses by 1900, each producing from 20 to 25 pounds of manure a day. Cobblestone streets were so thickly covered with the droppings of horses that the actual surface of the street was not visible for decades. Garbage was thrown out windows into the center of the streets, where free-roaming hogs were expected to take care of it, adding their own wastes in return. Regarding the stench created by the legions of hogs roaming Kansas City, the visiting Oscar Wilde observed that "it made granite eyes weep." Garbage was collected haphazardly. Few neighborhoods were free of the smells of tanneries and slaughterhouses. As industrialization spread, clouds of sulfurous, soot-laden smoke billowed from forests of smokestacks in every city. To disparage the pollution was considered poor form, as it symbolized prosperity. Some doctors even claimed that breathing smoke that contained carbon, sulfur and iodine might cure lung diseases and malaria. In 1881 New York was described as a "nasal disaster" with an atmosphere redolent of sulfur, ammonia gases, offal rendering, bone boiling, manure heaps, putrid animal wastes, fish scraps, kerosene, acid fumes, phosphate fertilizer and sludge. As bad as New York was, many considered Chicago even worse. "Having seen it...I desire urgently never to see it again. Its air is dirt," remarked Rudyard Kipling.

There has been talk in the Republican congress of deregulating those who would wish to keep herds of free-roaming hogs and turn back the clock in our major cities, but so far, no action.

URINE IS SMELLY AND FULL OF GERMS

Urine is normally odorless when it leaves the body. The foul smell is emitted by bacteria that set up housekeeping in it when it sits stagnant.

Far from carrying germs, the urine of a healthy person is actually sterile when it leaves the body. In an emergency, it is safer to use urine to clean a wound than to use water from a questionable source. Folk remedies have traditionally employed urine as a mild antiseptic to treat athlete's foot and external ear infections.

In the opening scene of *Waterworld*, the character played by Kevin Costner shocked audiences by drinking his own urine. We have heard of people doing this to survive in desperate circumstances, but there are others who do it as a matter of course. For thousands of years Indian yogis have practiced *amaroli*, a ritual that involves drinking a cup of their urine each morning after rising. It contains a hormone, melatonin, which has sedative properties and which the yogis believe is helpful in meditation. Always attuned to the wisdom of the East, many of our own New Agers have taken up urine therapy. *The Utne Reader*, in an article titled "It's Not Just for Flushing Anymore," reported that some enthusiasts drink their entire daily output. Bottoms up!

W. C. FIELDS' EPITAPH READS: "ON THE WHOLE, I'D RATHER BE IN PHILADELPHIA"

Somewhere along the line, we've all heard that carved on W. C. Fields' headstone is the wry objection, "On the whole, I'd rather be in Philadelphia."

The vault containing W. C. Fields' ashes actually reads, "W. C. Fields, 1880-1946." The gag line first appeared in a 1925 *Vanity Fair* humor feature on celebrity epitaphs. The story is just too good to die.

W. C. FIELDS SAID, "ANY MAN WHO HATES CHILDREN AND DOGS CAN'T BE ALL BAD"

This may be the most famous line associated with W. C. Fields, but he never said it. It was said *about* him by humorist Leo Rosten as he introduced the comedian at the 1939 Masquers banquet in Los Angeles. The joke brought the house down and was widely repeated. At the time few had heard of Rosten, so the gag was attributed to Fields himself.

That's the thing about classic witticisms: It's not enough that they be funny—

who they're attributed to is just as important. A line may get an immediate laugh if we picture Groucho Marx, W. C. Fields or Mae West delivering it, but not if its author is unknown. Many great lines are attributed to the people we can imagine saying them, whether or not they actually did.

Despite his reputation, in his will Fields left funds to found an orphanage—with the stipulation that it teach no religion.

WALT DISNEY DREW MICKEY MOUSE; DISNEY'S BODY WAS FROZEN AFTER HIS DEATH

Most people think of Walt Disney as the cartoonist behind Mickey Mouse and assume he only retired his pencil when his creation got

so big he could no longer handle the work. While it's true that Disney came up with the idea for Mickey, established his personality (if you call that a personality) and provided his voice early on, he did not draw Mickey in any of the cartoons, and throughout his life was frustrated by his inability to render even a passable likeness of the rodent. Walt was a visionary businessman, but his friend and collaborator Ub Iwerks had the artistic talent.

Even stranger than the idea that Walt Disney could draw is the persistent rumor that he ordered that his body be frozen after his death. Supposedly, it would be thawed out at some time when his lung cancer could be cured, or perhaps when his brain could be transplanted into one of those mechanical hillbilly bears in Frontierland. William Poundstone's *Big Secrets* reveals that Disney's body was cremated on December 17, 1966, at Forest Lawn cemetery, two days after his death.

WAR HAS BEEN THE LEADING CAUSE OF VIOLENT DEATH IN THE TWENTIETH CENTURY

With all the wars of the twentieth century, it's hard to believe that war did not kill more people than any other unnatural cause, but according to *Death by Government*, by R. J. Rummel, a political science professor at the University of Hawaii, that is not the case. So far this century international and civil wars have taken about 39 million lives. During the same period, 170 million people have

been done in by their own governments. Between 1917 and 1987 the Soviet Union murdered approximately 61.9 million of its citizens. Between 1949 and 1987, mostly under Chairman Mao, China killed 38.7 million. Hitler's Germany comes in third, with 21 million. Turkey killed some 2 million Armenians between 1909 and 1918, and Cambodia's Khmer Rouge killed some 2 million in the 1970s. Lesser known genocides include those of Pakistan, 1.5 million; Tito's Yugoslavia, 1 million; and Mexico, which between 1900 and 1920 murdered about 1.5 million Mexicans.

Sobering. You're more likely to be killed by your own government than by anyone else's.

WASHINGTON CHOPPED DOWN THE CHERRY TREE; THREW A SILVER DOLLAR ACROSS THE POTOMAC; WAS THE FIRST PRESIDENT; HIS BIRTHDAY IS FEBRUARY 22

There may be someone out there who hasn't gotten the news, so we'd better break this gently: Young George Washington did not chop down his father's favorite cherry tree, then bravely and truthfully admit the deed and receive a warm embrace for his honesty. The fact that this fable is still recounted to schoolchildren is amazing, as if a *World Weekly News* report about Bill Clinton's extraterrestrial half-brother would someday be the best-known fact about him. The story about George and the cherry tree first appeared in a fanciful biography written by Parson Mason Locke Weems. Parson Weems was something of an entrepreneur, and after Washington's death suggested to a publisher that there was "a great deal of money lying in the bones of old George." To get at some of that money, Weems wrote *The Life of George Washington with Curious Anecdotes, Equally Honorable to Himself and Exemplary to His Young Countrymen*. Published in 1800, the book sold so well it went through 21 reprintings in Weems' lifetime. Interestingly, the story about George and the cherry tree wasn't inserted until the fifth edition, published in 1806. Since then it has been repeated in any number of children's books about Washington.

In the original version George doesn't actually chop down the cherry tree, but "tried the edge of his hatchet" on it and barked it "so terribly, I don't believe the tree ever got the better of it."

If the news about the cherry tree wasn't traumatic enough, there's an even more alarming piece of information about our first President: George Washington was not actually born on Washington's birthday. It gets worse—he was actually born on February 11, Lincoln's birthday, only of course Lincoln hadn't been born yet. The whole mess is due to the fact that in 1732, when Washington was born, Great Britain and its colonies still followed the Julian calendar. Only when George Washington turned 20 was the switch made to the reformed Gregorian calendar, bumping his birthday up to February 22. This must have been confusing enough, but imagine if Washington were alive today and had to settle for the closest Monday, whatever the date might be.

Equally alarming is the fact that George Washington was not our first President, technically speaking. In 1781, Maryland finally signed the Articles of Confederation and the original 13 states formed a union. The assembled delegates then elected John Hanson, of Maryland, President of the United States in Congress Assembled, 1781. George Washington himself addressed Hanson as President of the United States in his reply to Hanson's letter of congratulation upon Washington's victory at Yorktown. Hanson served a one-year term, and seven others also presided over the Congress by 1789, when the Constitution was ratified and George Washington was elected President. In a nit-picking sense, he was the *ninth* American President rather than the first.

Washington had lost all his teeth by middle age and until the end of his life, between fighting a revolution and leading the nation, he pursued a futile quest for properly fitting dentures. His false teeth may have given him pains, but never splinters—contrary to rumor, they were not made from wood, but from walrus ivory and hammered gold.

He also never threw a silver dollar across the Potomac. The U.S. had no dollar until 1792, four years before Washington's death.

Some may be surprised to learn that Washington was unusually tall for his day; perhaps six foot three, nearly as tall as Abraham Lincoln and Bill Clinton.

WASPS AND HORNETS DIE AFTER THEY STING

As children, most of us felt some modest satisfaction when we heard that the wasp or hornet that stung us paid with its life. Unfortunately, nature does not always live up to a child's idea of justice. It's true that the honeybee dies after it stings (its barbed stinger sticks in the victim's skin, pulling out the bee's entrails with it), but honeybees don't sting unless they are severely provoked. The more trigger-happy wasps and hornets can sting many times without paying any price.

WATER ALWAYS SPIRALS DOWN THE DRAIN COUNTERCLOCKWISE IN THE NORTHERN HEMISPHERE

It's a bit of pseudo-science that water, spiraling out of a drain, always flows counterclockwise in the Northern Hemisphere and clockwise in the Southern Hemisphere. This consistent movement is attributed to the Coriolis force, the force that the earth's rotation exerts on moving objects. There really is such a force—it explains prevailing winds and the different rotational direction of hurricanes in the two hemispheres, among other things. Water whirlpooling down a drain is another matter, far too insignificant to be affected one way or the other by the earth's movement. The direction of its spiral depends on the shape of the drain and the water currents set up as the basin was filled.

A WEAK CHIN INDICATES A WEAK PERSONALITY

Physiognomy is the pseudo-science that associates character traits with facial features. Aristotle was an early believer; he thought that a person who resembled a particular animal would have a similar temperament; for example, a "bulldog jaw" would indicate tenacity. It's hard to shake this feeling, because Hollywood constantly reinforces it with stereotypical casting. When you see that lean, silver-haired, pinstripe-suited, jut-jawed guy striding confidently up Fifth Avenue, you probably assume he's the CEO of some great corporation rather than a sales rep for that short, fat, bald guy shuffling along behind him. History cautions against this assumption. Some of the most forceful figures of all time have triumphed over their receding chins. Weak-chinned Frederick the Great was a brilliant eighteenth-century military campaigner who greatly expanded Prussia's size and power. The English general James Wolfe, who was wounded three times—the third time fatally—while commanding the British army that conquered Quebec, was a chinless wonder if there ever was one. Queen Victoria, certainly in no need of assertiveness training, also displayed the molelike profile.

WEBSTER'S DICTIONARIES ARE
LATER EDITIONS OF THE ORIGINAL

Noah Webster's name has been synonymous with dictionaries since he put together the first American dictionary in the early 1800s. However, the name Webster on a dictionary does not necessarily mean that it has anything to do with the original. Titles and names cannot be copyrighted, so any low-rent publisher who wants to put out a dictionary is free to attach the prestigious Webster name to it.

Noah Webster's dictionaries helped to establish the differences between American and British spelling. One of his innovations was to include slang and jargon, but he refused to permit any of the taboo words in his volumes, no doubt anticipating the hours schoolchildren would waste searching for anything they could get a giggle out of. Webster later published a version of the Bible that omitted all the dirty parts.

Interestingly, Noah Webster did not use his own name in the title of his dictionary. It was called *An American Dictionary of the English Language*.

Webster died on May 28, 1843. His last words were *zymosis*, *zymurgy* and *zyzzyva*.

"WE DON'T NEED NO STINKIN' BADGES!" WAS A LINE IN *TREASURE OF SIERRA MADRE*

Despite the fact that that's the way everyone remembers the line, it's not what the Mexican bandits said to Bogart. The bandit leader told Bogart that he and his men were Federales, or mounted police. When Bogart asked to see their badges, the bandit replied, "Badges? We ain't got no badges. We don't need no badges. I don't have to show you any stinking badges!"

WHAT'S IN A NAME?

Banana oil has nothing to do with the fruit. It's a petroleum chemical that smells like bananas, and is used in lacquers and glues.

Buttermilk does not contain butter. It is a by-product of the butter-making process and actually contains less fat than ordinary milk.

Centipedes, despite their name, do not necessarily have one hundred legs, but anywhere from 28 to 354 depending on the species. Neither do millipedes have a thousand legs.

The century plant does not bloom every hundred years. In favorable climates, it blooms every five to ten years, though they have been known to require as long as sixty.

Chalk, as is used on blackboards, is not chalk. It is plaster of Paris.

Corned beef has nothing to do with the grain we call corn. Corn has traditionally referred to large, coarse grains or seeds, in this case "corns" of salt, or rock salt, that is used to preserve the beef.

Electric eels are not eels, but a South American freshwater fish related to the carp.

Head cheese is pretty cheesy stuff, but it's not a dairy product. It is chopped and boiled meat from the head and feet of a pig, mixed with gelatin and pressed into the shape of a cheese.

Heartburn has nothing to do with the heart, but is caused by stomach acid irritating the lower esophagus.

Horned toads are not toads but lizards.

Horseshoe crabs are not crabs. They are the survivors of an order which died out 175 million years ago. Their closest existing relatives are the scorpion and the spider.

Koala bears are not related to bears—they are marsupials, like kangaroos and opossums.

Panda bears likewise bear no relation to bruins. They are in a family of their own.

Lead pencils have no lead in them, only graphite.

Pigskins, as footballs are often called, are not made from pigskin, but cowhide.

Rice paper is not made from rice, but from the pith of a tree in the ginseng family.

Sugarplums, as mentioned in Clement Moore's *The Night Before Christmas*, and Tchaikovsky's "Nutcracker Suite", have nothing to do with plums. They are hard candies.

Ten-gallon hats do not even hold one gallon. Three quarts is about the max. The ego of the head inside may be immeasurable.

Two-by-fours do not measure two by four inches, but 1 3/4 inches by 3 1/2 inches. The board is sized before planing, smoothing, and drying.

Welsh rabbit, or sometimes Welsh rarebit, is no threat to the bunny population. It's just a snide name for melted cheese on toast, similar to "Scotch broth," which when applied to a glass of water was once considered a real knee-slapper.

Whalebone, one of the coveted products of the nineteenth-century whaling industry, is not bone at all. It is keratin, similar to our fingernails. It comes from the fringed plates attached to the upper jaw of the baleen whale, which the whale uses to strain plankton out of seawater. Mankind put it to more important purposes, as umbrella ribs and corset stays.

"WHAT IS GOOD FOR GENERAL MOTORS IS GOOD FOR THE COUNTRY" WAS AN EXPRESSION OF CORPORATE ARROGANCE

It must be a strange experience. You've risen to the top of your field and have received national recognition for your abilities. Then, as if to seal your success, the President of the United States taps you for a high-level appointment. Flushed with pride and confidence, you head to Washington to begin your duties, with only a perfunctory confirmation hearing to get past. Then, for reasons entirely beyond your control, perhaps even beyond your comprehension, you are turned into a political football, tossed around, kicked a few times and in most cases sent back home, deflated. We've seen it a lot lately, but it's been going on for years.

In 1953 Charles E. Wilson quit his $600,000 a year salary as president of General Motors to take a $22,000 a year post as Eisenhower's Secretary of Defense. At General Motors, Wilson had been known for his progressive policies, working cooperatively with the United Automobile Workers' union. He even instituted an employee pension fund, despite being warned that workers would invest their capital and come to be the owners of American businesses. "Exactly what they should be," Wilson said.

If life were fair, wrote John Steele Gordon in American Heritage, liberals would hail Charlie Wilson as a hero. However, in 1953, with the inauguration of Eisenhower after 20 years of Democratic presidents, liberals were in a surly mood, especially about all the businessmen that were being put into cabinet positions. At his confirmation hearing, Wilson was asked if he could make a decision that would be good for America but not necessarily good for General Motors. Trying to strike just the right note, Wilson answered, "Yes sir, I could. I cannot conceive of one because for years I thought what was good for our country was good for General Motors, and vice versa." From the closed hearing room, Democratic committee members leaked Wilson's response to the press as "What is good for General Motors is good for the country."

This misquote entered *Bartlett's Familiar Quotations* and is perhaps the ultimate expression of smug corporate arrogance. Charlie Wilson performed well as Secretary of Defense, but remains best known for something he never said.

WHERE DID THEY COME FROM? CHINESE CHECKERS; CHOP SUEY; ENGLISH HORN; ENGLISH MUFFINS; FORTUNE COOKIES; FRENCH FRIES; FRENCH POODLES; GUINEA PIGS; INDIA INK; JORDAN ALMONDS; PHILADELPHIA BRAND CREAM CHEESE; PINEAPPLES

—Chinese checkers did not originate in China, but in England. The game, played with marbles on a star-shaped board, became popular in America and Japan before the Chinese ever heard of it.

—Chop suey was unknown in China. Some say it was invented by Chinese chefs who worked in the gold fields of California and cooked with whatever ingredients were at hand. Others credit it to either a New York or a San Francisco chef. The name is supposed to be an Americanization of *tsa-sui*, Chinese for "odds and ends."

—The English horn is neither English nor a horn. It originated in the Near East, was developed in Vienna, and is a woodwind.

—English muffins are popular in the states, but if you order them at a London breakfast shop you'll draw a blank look. What we call English muffins are unknown in the British Isles.

—Fortune Cookies, the traditional conclusion to a Chinese dinner, were created by a Chinese chef in America. They are unknown in China.

—If you figure that french fries didn't come from France, you probably guessed they were the proud product of American junk-food technology. Actually, according to Tom Burnham's *Dictionary of Misinformation*, they originated in Belgium in the nineteenth century, and were sold on the street in paper cones as *patates frites*.

—French poodles were originally bred in Germany, not in France.

—Guinea pigs are not pigs but rodents, and they did not originate in Guinea (West Africa). They are native to South America.

— India ink is actually from China; the French call it Chinese ink.

—Jordan almonds didn't come from Jordan, but from Spain. Its name was originally *jardyne almande*, or "garden almond." The confection has been around since the Renaissance.

—Philadelphia Brand cream cheese was not originally manufactured in the fabled City of Brotherly Love, but rather in New York. The "Philadelphia" moniker was intended to exploit the reputation for fine food that that city once enjoyed.

—As closely as the pineapple is identified with Hawaii, the fruit was not native to the Pacific islands. It was discovered in the Caribbean by Columbus, who gave it its odd name because of its resemblance to a pine cone. It was first introduced to Hawaii in 1790, and serious cultivation began about a hundred years ago. Today Hawaii produces most of the world's pineapples.

WHISKY WARMS YOU UP

Booze gives you a warm feeling, so it may seem helpful to have a nip when you're out in the cold. In fact, this can be the worst thing a severely chilled person can do. Alcohol dilates the tiny capillaries near the surface of the skin. Since the skin is where the body's warmth-sensing nerves are located, this may make you *feel* warm for a few

moments but it actually speeds heat loss from your body. In a survival situation, drinking alcohol can accelerate your death from hypothermia. So if you're ever trapped by an avalanche in the Alps and you're found by one of those St. Bernards with a little barrel of brandy on his collar, be advised that he doesn't have your best interests at heart.

(Be advised you're also losing your mind. Though the monks at the Hospice of the St. Bernard Pass in the Swiss Alps used to employ St. Bernards to help locate lost travelers, they never equipped them with a little cask of brandy.)

WHISTLER PAINTED "WHISTLER'S MOTHER"

One of the most famous American paintings, now hanging in the Louvre in Paris, shows a grim older woman seated in profile. The painting was indeed of the artist's mother, Anna McNeill Whistler, but it was not titled "Whistler's Mother." James Whistler called it "Arrangement in Gray and Black. No. 1." Once it became popular, he retitled it "Portrait of My Mother."

Whistler's work was not universally admired during his lifetime. One critic, John Ruskin, called it impudent of him to "ask two hundred guineas for flinging a pot of paint in the public's face."

WHITE WINE IS MADE FROM WHITE GRAPES

The supermarket offers a choice between pale green and deep purple grapes, and wine merchants purvey both white and red wines, so it's only logical to assume that the white wine is made from the lighter grapes. In fact, it may or may not be—the inside of a grape imparts no color to the wine. What vintners call "black" grapes (those whose color ranges from red to bluish black) are routinely used to make white wine—all that it requires is that the grape skins be removed before fermenting. This process is called *blanche de noir*—white from black. Wine skins contain color pigments, anthocyanins, that give wine its color. If the skins are left in for part of the winemaking process, they give the blush or rosé tint; they are left in throughout to produce red wine.

THE WILD WEST WAS A PLACE OF MURDER AND MAYHEM

Whenever there is a discussion of crime, violence and the prevalence of guns in our society, someone is sure to observe that "it won't be long till we're back to the days of the Wild West," implying that that would be a lot worse than what we have now.

It is true that in most western towns nearly everyone carried a gun. While Mark Twain worked at a newspaper in the notorious mining town of Aurora, Nevada, he wore a revolver "in deference to popular sentiment, and in order that I might not, by its absence, be offensively conspicuous, and a subject of remark." Nevertheless, the crime levels then pale to what we see today. Roger McGrath, professor of history at UCLA, has made a study of the frontier town of Aurora. It might have been expected to be one of the most violent places imaginable, with a transient population of over 5,000 mostly single young males. Some had struck it rich, others had not. The town was loaded with brothels and bars (one for every 25 residents) that ran 24 hours a day. Law enforcement was unreliable. Yet muggings were rare—fewer than 20 in its boom years of 1861 through 1865. (Most of our American cities today average 30 to 40 times as much robbery and theft per capita.) Stagecoaches

were robbed of their strongboxes a couple of dozen times, but only twice were the passengers robbed. There were no bank robberies. There were no reported rapes; what little violence was committed against women was suffered by prostitutes. A man who assaulted a "respectable" woman wouldn't have lived long. Even swearing in front of a woman was punishable by a fine and a month in jail. During the boom years there were around five homicides a year in Aurora, most of them in barrooms between drunks defending their honor. "Duels" of this sort were legal and not of much concern to decent folks. Only one innocent citizen was killed in cold blood, and his murderer was promptly hanged. This murder rate, though high, pales compared to that of Washington, D.C.

The figures on Aurora are not atypical. 1878 was Dodge City's deadliest year, with a total of five killings—fewer than you'd expect before the opening credits of the average Clint Eastwood western. The worst year in Tombstone also saw five deadly shootings, and historian W. Eugene Hollon observes that the only reason the shoot-out at the O.K. Corral became so famous was that the town played it up to attract settlers, and later, tourists.

Most of the well-known gunfighters of the Old West didn't kill as many men as they liked people to believe—an inflated reputation was useful to them. Billy the Kid didn't gun down "twenty-one men before he was twenty-one"; he killed three for certain and perhaps

185

three or four more. When a reporter asked how many men he had killed, Wild Bill Hickock answered, "I would be willing to take my oath on the Bible tomorrow that I have killed over one hundred," and that was not including Indians. In fact his body count totaled three, all unarmed. Bat Masterson is believed by some to have killed three; by others, none. Wyatt Earp's reputation rests mostly on the O.K. Corral. On the other hand, there are lesser-known killers such as John Wesley Hardin who dispatched 44.

The idea that a gunslinger could have terrorized a western town is pure Hollywood. The people that relocated west were not easily cowed; many were veterans of the Civil War and, of course, armed. *The Vigilantes of Montana* recounts the sorry end of one would-be town terrorizer, Jack Slade. Backed up by his gang, the notorious ruffian raised hell in a mining town and then tore up a subpoena the sheriff served him. The sheriff rounded up 600 armed miners (not that many were needed, but no one wanted to miss out) and they marched Slade to a makeshift gibbet. A gang member announced that the crowd would have to kill him before it would kill his friend, but when a hundred cocked weapons were instantly pointed at him,

he withdrew the sentiment. Faced with the gallows, Slade began to blubber. "He didn't die game," snorted a miner scornfully.

There is also no case on record of a showdown at high noon on a western street.

The image we have of the West was created by the penny novels and the Buffalo Bill Wild West Show; it continues to live in film and fiction because it provides such a suitable backdrop for the telling of dramatic tales.

WILLIAM TELL SHOT AN APPLE OFF HIS SON'S HEAD

William Tell, the great thirteenth-century hero of Swiss independence, did not shoot an apple off his son's head with a crossbow. He couldn't have. He did not have a son, a crossbow, an apple or, in fact, an existence outside of the imagination of an anonymous fifteenth-century storyteller.

The Swiss take enormous patriotic pride in William Tell and

have even built a chapel over the spot where he is supposed to have lived. Suggestions that he was a mythic character are not taken kindly; one visiting scholar who expressed his doubts was threatened with death. The Swiss are a heavily armed people and it's probably best not to needle them.

Every nation has its folk heroes, and it's sometimes surprising to find that some of the most unlikely ones actually existed—Johnny Appleseed, Casey Jones and John Henry, for example. The tale of William Tell, though, in all its dramatic detail, is a complete fiction.

WILLIE SUTTON SAID, "I ROB BANKS BECAUSE THAT'S WHERE THE MONEY IS"

When asked by a reporter why he robbed banks, Willie Sutton is supposed to have answered, "Because that's where the money is." The quote is often used, for example, when discussing such matters as why budget-cutting politicians go after Social Security— "because that's where the money is," of course.

It's a great quote, but Willie Sutton never said it. In his autobiography, he wrote, "The credit belongs to some enterprising reporter who apparently felt a need to fill out his copy. I can't even remember when I first read it. It just seemed to appear one day, and then it was everywhere."

WITCHES WERE BURNED IN SALEM

Arthur Miller's *The Crucible* is a staple of high school English courses, and it impressed most of us with the idea that the persecution of witches was a mania peculiar to seventeenth-century New England, revealing the dark, repressive underside of the American character. This impression was intentional on Miller's part—his play was not really about witchcraft, but about post-World War II McCarthyism. The persecution of purely fictitious "witches" provided a useful metaphor for Leftists and Communists who were under attack in the 1940s and 1950s.

First of all, it should be noted that belief in witches was not evidence of hysteria in some remote outpost. In the sixteenth through eighteenth centuries, virtually everyone in Christendom took the existence of witches very much for granted.

The year 1692 was the time of the notorious witch trials in

Salem, Massachusetts. One hundred and fifty people were arrested, of whom 50 confessed to practicing witchcraft. Of these, 30 were nonetheless acquitted, while 20 were convicted and executed as witches. Contrary to popular belief, it wasn't only women—men, boys and even dogs were as likely to be accused. Of those executed, none were burned—19 were hanged and one, Giles Corey, was crushed to death for refusing to enter a plea. Corey's steadfast defiance even as he underwent torture helped dampen the community's enthusiasm for the witch hunts. There were 10 others convicted but not put to death. Two dogs were executed.

Witch trials were by no means confined to New England. Rebecca Fowler was hanged as a witch in Maryland in 1685, and in 1706 a Virginia woman was tried as a witch and released. Several people in South Carolina were punished for practicing witchcraft. Outside of Salem, only 16 witches were executed in the American colonies. Twenty years after the hysteria there was serious contrition over the episode. Massachusetts officially cleared the names of all of those accused of witchcraft, and the legislature provided compensation to the heirs of those executed.

To put this in perspective, it should be noted that during the sixteenth and seventeenth centuries in Europe, hundreds of thousands of people were burned as witches. In France, 900 were incinerated in a single city and 5,000 in one province. England put the match to some 30,000. By some estimates *500,000* people were burned as witches in Europe between the fifteenth and seventeenth centuries, and the practice did not end until well into the "enlightened" eighteenth century. Rather than ask why the American colonists were so swept up in the witch-hunting craze, it might be more interesting to find out why they were largely immune to it.

WOMEN EARN 59 CENTS FOR EVERY DOLLAR A MAN MAKES

This figure has been in circulation since the 1970s and still frequently cited despite the fact that it is long outdated. In 1990, the *New York Times* reported that the current figure for women's earnings was close to 72¢ against a man's dollar. That still may not sound equitable, but the *Times* points out that it looks worse than it is because it includes older women who work only parttime, such as "the mother who graduated from high school, left the work force at twenty, and returned to a minimum wage at a local store." Depending on the age bracket, single women earn between 93 and 106% of what a man makes with a comparable education and work history.

According to a recent report, among working couples 50% of the women earn roughly the same as their husbands, and 25% earn more.

Whatever the disparities in wages, it should be noted that women own about 70 to 80% of the nation's wealth. The elderly are the richest sector of our population, controlling most of the property and assets. Since the men tend to die off seven years earlier than their widows, they leave them holding the swag.

THE WOODSTOCK FESTIVAL WAS HELD IN WOODSTOCK, NEW YORK

As Mecca is to Moslems, so Woodstock is to rock 'n' rollers. It's the magnetic pole of the sixties rock scene, the place where the magic really happened. So it seems somewhat odd that, to this day, there has never been a rock festival in the town of Woodstock, New York.

The 1969 Woodstock Festival was held was meant to be held in that artsy town where Bob Dylan and The Band owned homes, and promoters took the name for their production company, Woodstock Ventures. However, due to problems there and elsewhere, they eventually ended up at Max Yasgur's farm in Bethell, New York, 40 miles away.

In 1994, there were two separate 25th anniversary concerts, neither of which took place in the town of Woodstock. "Bethel '94" was held on Yasgur's farm, while "Woodstock '94," the large, corporate-sponsored event, took place in Saugerties, New York.

XMAS IS A RECENT, DISRESPECTFUL ABBREVIATION OF CHRISTMAS

The use of the word *Xmas* instead of *Christmas* has struck many Christians as a sad commentary on the secularization of the religious holiday. Xmas is not a modern coinage, however, and was never intended disrespectfully. The abbreviation X for *Christ* has been used since the twelfth century. *X* is the first letter of Christ's name in Greek, XPICTOC as it is written, and the first two letters, *XP*, often appear on church vestments and religious articles. As an abbreviation for Christmas, Xmas has been dated as far back as 1755.

It is believed that it is this *X* that gives us the Christian symbol of the cross and not the structure on which Christ was crucified. The Romans used a T-shaped structure for crucifixions.

YAWNS BRING IN EXTRA OXYGEN

Though it would seem obvious that a great wheezing, arm-stretching, mouth-gaping, tonsil-exposing yawn is just the thing to recharge your weary system with a dose of oxygen, that's not what a yawn gives you. According to researchers at the University of Maryland, the amount of oxygen taken in during a six-second yawn is less than would be taken in were you to breathe normally for the same period. You lose oxygen, rather than gain it, when you yawn. So what's the point? Apparently, it's a gestalt thing. The whole exercise just makes you feel good.

YOU CAN ALWAYS TELL WHEN YOU'RE BEING STARED AT

Most men learn this the hard way. They think they're in a safe vantage point from which to gawk at a beautiful woman, only to have her shoot them a withering glance.

Despite what we think, and what our experience seems to tell us, experiments have proven that we have no special ability to sense the fact that others are looking at us. We may think that we do, but it's one of those cases of selective memory, such as "it always rains after you wash the car."

Experiments in Psychical Research, published in 1917 by Stanford psychologist John Edgar Coover, covers the matter in a chapter titled "The Feeling of Being Stared at." Of his students, 77% claimed they could tell when someone was staring at them. One by one, he sat them with their backs toward him. He sat at a desk, rolling a die. On an even number, he stared. On an odd, he closed his eyes and imagined a landscape. Every 15 seconds, the students would guess whether he was staring or not. If their guesses were purely random, their odds would be 50-50. If they guessed correctly in a significant majority of the cases, some psychic phenomenon would seem to be at work.

There were 1,000 guesses in all.

Of these, 502 were correct.

YOU CAN'T TICKLE YOURSELF

Does tickling only work if it is done by another person? Darwin thought so, arguing that "the precise point to be tickled must not be known." To prove otherwise, just try stroking the roof of your mouth with your finger.

EVERYTHING YOU KNOW IS **WRONG**

BIBLIOGRAPHY

Achenbach, Joel. Why Things Are. Ballantine Books: New York, 1991

Adams, Cecil. The Straight Dope. Chicago Review Press: Chicago, 1984

Adams, Cecil. More of the Straight Dope. Ballantine Books: New York, 1988

Adams, Cecil. The Return of the Straight Dope. Ballantine Books: New York, 1994

Bettman, Otto. The Good Old Days—They Were Terrible! Random House: New York, 1974

Blumberg, Rhoda and Leda. The Simon and Schuster Book of Facts and Fallacies. Julian Messner, a division of Simon & Schuster, Inc.: New York, 1983

Booler, Jr., Paul F. and George, John. They Never Said It: A Book of Fake Quotes, Misquotes, and Misleading Attributions. Oxford University Press: New York, 1989

Burnham, Tom. The Dictionary of Misinformation. Thomas Y. Crowell, Publishers: New York, 1975

Burnham, Tom. More Misinformation. Lippincott & Crowell, Publishers: New York, 1980

Castle, Sue. Old Wives' Tales. A Citadel Press Book, published by the Carol Publishing Group: New York, 1992

Chamberlain, Wilt. A View From Above. Villard Books: New York, 1991

Dickson, Paul, and Goulden, Joseph. Myth-Informed. Putnam Publishing Group: New York, 1993.

Dunnigan, James. Dirty Little Secrets: Military Information You're Not Supposed to Know. William Morrow and Company, Inc.: New York, 1990

Dunnigan, James and Nofi, Albert. Dirty Little Secrets of World War II: Military Information No One Told You About the Greatest, Most Terrible War in History. William Morrow and Company, Inc.: New York, 1994

Ehrlich, Robert. The Cosmological Milkshake. Rutgers University Press: New Brunswick, N.J., 1994

Encyclopaedia Britannica, Inc. Encyclopaedia Britannica. Chicago, 1987

Gallant, Roy. Our Universe. National Geographic: Washington, D.C. 1986.

Gilovich, Thomas. How We Know What Isn't So: The Fallability of Human Reason in Everyday Life. The Free Press: New York, 1991

Goldberg, M. Hirsh. The Book of Lies. William Morrow and Company, Inc.: New York, 1990 ·

Goldberg, M. Hirsh. The Complete Book of Greed. William Morrow and Company, Inc.: New York, 1994

Hawke, David Freeman. Everyday Life in Early America. Harper & Row: New York, 1988

Irish, Prothro, Richardson. The Politics of American Democracy. Prentice-Hall, Inc.: Englewood Cliffs, New Jersey, 1981

Johnson, Ferris. The Encyclopedia of Popular Misconceptions. A Citadel Press Book, published by the Carol Publishing Group: New York, 1994

Keyes, Ralph. "Nice Guys Finish Seventh": False Phrases, Spurious Sayings, and Familiar Misquotations.

HarperCollins, Publishers, Inc.: New York, 1992

Kohn, Alfie. You Know What They Say…: The Truth About Popular Beliefs. HarperCollins Publishers, Inc.: New York, 1990

Kopel, David B. The Samurai, the Mountie, and the Cowboy. A Cato Institute Book. Prometheus Books: Buffalo, New York, 1992

Lane, Mark. Rush to Judgment. Fawcett Publications: New York, 1967

Menninger, Bonar. Mortal Error: The Shot That Killed JFK. St. Martin's Press: New York, 1992

Montagu, Ashley and Darling, Edward. The Prevalence of Nonsense. Harper and Row, Publishers: New York, 1967

Moore, Laurence. Lightning Never Strikes Twice and Other False Facts. Avon Books: New York, 1994

Morris, Scot. The Book of Strange Facts and Useless Information. Doubleday & Company: Garden City, New York, 1979

O'Rourke, P. J. All the Trouble in the World. The Atlantic Monthly Pree: New York, 1994

Panati, Charles. Panati's Extraordinary Endings of Practically Everything and Everybody. Harper & Row: New York, 1989

Panati, Charles. Panati's Extraordinary Origins of Practically Everything and Everybody. Harper & Row: New York, 1987

Posner, Gerald. Case Closed: Lee Harvey Oswald and the Assassination of JFK. Random House: New York, 1993

Poundstone, William. Big Secrets. William Morrow & Company, Inc.: New York, 1983

Pullum, Geoffrey K. The Great Eskimo Vocabulary Hoax and Other Irreverent Essays on the Study of Language. University of Chicago Press, 1991

Rawson, Hugh. Devious Derivations. Crown Publishers, Inc.: New York, 1994

Rosenblatt, Roger. Life Itself; Abortion in the American Mind. Random House: New York, 1992

Rosenbloom, Joseph. Bananas Don't Grow on Trees. Sterling Publishing Company: New York, 1978

Shenkman, Richard. Legends, Lies & Cherished Myths of American History. William Morrow and Company, Inc.: New York, 1988

Shenkman, Richard. Legends, Lies & Cherished Myths of World History. HarperCollins Publishers, Inc.: New York, 1993

Taberner, P.V. Aphrodisiacs, the Science and the Myth. University of Pennsylvania Press: Philadelphia, 1985

Torrence, Bruce T. Hollywood, The First Hundred Years. New York Zoetrope: New York, 1982

Tuleja, Tad. Fabulous Fallacies: More Than 300 Popular Beliefs That Are Not True. Harmony Books: New York, 1982

Varasdi, J. Allen. Myth Information. Ballantine Books: New York, 1989

Wallace, Irving; Wallechinsky, David; Wallace, Amy. Significa. E. P. Dutton, Inc.: New York, 1983

Wicker, Tom. One of Us. Random House: New York, 1991

Wilson, James Q. American Government. D.C. Heath and Company: Lexington, Massachusetts, 1989